PUB WA
— IN —
Gloucesters

C000253423

Other areas covered in the Pub Walks series include:

Bedfordshire
Berkshire
Bristol and Bath
Buckinghamshire
Cheshire
The Chilterns
The Cotswolds
Dartmoor and South Devon
Derbyshire
Essex
Herefordshire
Hertfordshire
The Isle of Wight
Lancashire
Leicestershire and Rutland
Lincolnshire
Middlesex and West London

Norfolk
Northamptonshire
Nottinghamshire
Oxfordshire
Shropshire
Suffolk
Surrey
The Surrey Hills
The Thames Valley
North Wales*
South Wales
Warwickshire
Wiltshire
Worcestershire
East Yorkshire
North Yorkshire
South Yorkshire
West Yorkshire

*A complete catalogue is available from the publisher at
3 Catherine Road, Newbury, Berkshire.*

PUB WALKS
IN
Gloucestershire

THIRTY CIRCULAR WALKS
AROUND GLOUCESTERSHIRE INNS

Nigel Hammond

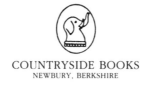

COUNTRYSIDE BOOKS
NEWBURY, BERKSHIRE

First Published 1994
© Nigel Hammond 1994

COUNTRYSIDE BOOKS
3 Catherine Road
Newbury, Berkshire

ISBN 1 85306 318 5

Designed by Mon Mohan
Cover illustration by Colin Doggett
Photographs by the author

Produced through MRM Associates Ltd., Reading
Typeset by Paragon Typesetters, Queensferry, Clwyd
Printed in England

Contents

Publisher's Note

We hope that you obtain considerable enjoyment from this book; great care has been taken in its preparation. However, changes of landlord and actual closures are sadly not uncommon. Likewise, although at the time of publication all routes followed public rights of way or well-established permitted paths, diversion orders can be made and permissions withdrawn.

We cannot of course be held responsible for such diversion orders and any resultant inaccuracies in the text which result from these or any other changes to the route nor any damage which might result from walkers trespassing on private property. We are anxious that all details covering both pubs and walks are kept up to date, and would therefore welcome information from readers which would be relevant to future editions.

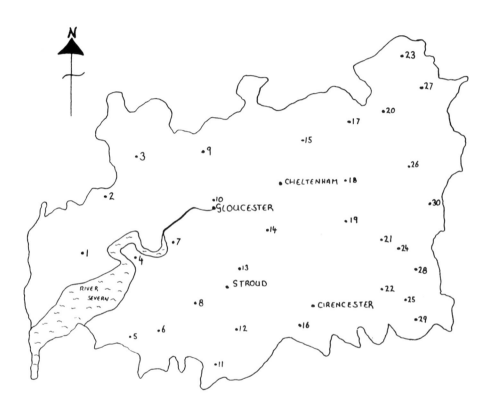

Area map showing locations of the walks.

Introduction

The walks in this book have been carefully chosen to take advantage of the variety of scenery there is for the walker in this charming and beautiful county of Gloucestershire. It is an area especially well-known for its great walking and herein you will find relatively short strolls, breezy walks on the Cotswolds, quiet walks by the Severn or woodland walks in the Forest of Dean.

The varied nature of the walking relates directly to the threefold division of the county itself. Most people will associate a picture of Gloucestershire with limestone Cotswolds. Here you will find many of the prettiest villages such as Bourton-on-the-Water, the Slaughters and Bibury, which are also very well-known tourist areas. However, it is easy to escape the crowds and discover remote and quiet countryside walks which, for the keen observer, will be full of wildlife and exude the scent of the wild flowers, the woodland and growing pasture. There is good ale and food to be had in characterful, friendly and sometimes unspoilt pubs in the Cotswolds, indeed throughout the county.

The Severn valley funnels down to a broad estuary and runs from the river's junction with the Avon at Tewkesbury into the estuary south of Berkeley: this is largely an area of pasture and some orchards. It is lush, green and picturesque, an area where the stone building materials of the Cotswolds give way to brick, pantiles and half-timbering.

On the west of the Severn is another superb area of natural beauty. The ancient Forest of Dean extends broadly from the Severn to the Wye: in its quiet glades you will find foxgloves and primroses hidden in the bracken and among the oak and beech trees. This is an area with a rich and varied history which has been highly valued for centuries for its timber, stone, coal and iron. Today you will find much peace and few crowds. Forest Enterprises has provided picnic sites, barbecues, car parks, viewpoints and waymarked trails for the walker in this truly magnificent setting.

Nearly 70% of the county by area lies east of a line through Gloucester and I have reflected that detail in this book. I have included walks varying from 2 miles up to 7 miles: some are easy rambles, others more demanding. Some are suitable for an afternoon walk after a pub lunch; but the longer walks are best attempted prior to taking refreshment.

The county has a wealth of fascinating inns and to select only 30 was not an easy task. Many good and suitable hostelries have of necessity to be left aside, some the more so when one adds the requirement that they should be located on a broadly circular walk in varied countryside.

Parking your car is always a difficulty. Many of the pubs selected have car parks or there is suitable parking nearby. Out of courtesy ask the landlord before you leave your car: some would like you to order your meal before you set off, particularly if you are a large party or family group, and such a request could work out for your mutual convenience. I have not mentioned the opening and mealtimes of all pubs included in these walks, but it is pretty standard and most seem to be taking a break between 3 pm and 6 pm, with last orders for lunch before 2 pm.

Wherever you park your car be sure to move all possessions into the boot: some parts of the county are more prone to car crime than others, but always be careful to minimize the risk.

The sketch maps accompanying the walks are provided for guidance only. To make it easy to see where the walks begin I have included the grid reference of the pub in question and have used the OS Landranger 1:50 000 map. Take a copy with you to provide further guidance for the route. It is also useful if you should want to shorten, amend or lengthen the walk. I always enjoy walking with the OS Pathfinder 1:25 000 map (2 ½ ins to the mile) for the superb detail it offers, and such a map covering the area of your intended walk would be ideal.

It is also a good plan to carry binoculars – to view the buzzards wheeling, the waterfowl feeding or the woodland birds flitting through the branches – but also to look across that long ploughed field in front of you where the path is indistinctly waymarked, to locate the stile or narrow exit on the other side. Finally, always wear suitable clothing for the season, taking into account the possibility of changing weather conditions during the day, together with a pair of good walking boots or shoes. Observe the Countryside Code, close gates behind you, keep dogs on the leash in fields with other animals, and take your litter home. Good walking, good drinking, good eating. Enjoy yourselves!

Nigel Hammond
Summer 1994

The Forest of Dean
The Speech House

The Speech House stands isolated between Cinderford and Coleford, close to the centre of the Forest of Dean. Built in 1676, it is an imposing building erected by the Crown when attempting to stop abuses of the forest. It contained two courts to deal with infringement of forest law. The Verderers Court dealt with poaching and oversaw the common privileges while the Court of Mine Law settled disputes among the mining community of the Forest of Dean. This old court house is now the Speech House Hotel: it has a small front bar which serves drink, bar food, and has substantial dining-rooms and accommodation. Although not the typical country pub, it is ideally located and walkers are made very welcome.

The draught beers include John Smith's Bitter, Courage Best Bitter, Foster's lager and Beamish Irish Stout. There is also draught Dry Blackthorn cider, John Smith's low calorie beer, LA and Kaliber.

The bar serves an extensive range of sandwiches, all consisting of a round and a half on white or brown bread. There are seven varieties for the less adventurous, including salad and smoked salmon. For the more adventurous there are, specially made to order and subject to availability, cold bacon and eggs; ham and coleslaw; curried chicken and mayonnaise; beef, horseradish and beetroot; Madeira-marinated herring and mackerel paste and lemon.

Other bar food includes home-made seasonal soup and roll, chicken and pork pâté, cold meat platter, Cumberland sausage and granary bap with sweet pickle, vegetable lasagne, Stilton ploughman's, coffee or tea. There are also special dishes of the day and the day's choice is advertised separately on a blackboard.

Telephone: Dean (0594) 822607.

How to get there: The Speech House Hotel is at the heart of the Forest of Dean on the B4226, virtually halfway between Coleford and Cinderford. There is also a minor road running north to the Speech House from the B4431 at Moseley Green 2 miles away.

Parking: Car parks are available at the front and side of the Speech House, also in the courtyard at the rear. The walk starts a few hundred yards away from the hotel and there is an extensive car park at the forest trail at the south of New Beechenhurst Inclosure on the B4226, just east of the Speech House.

Length of the walk: 4 miles. Map: OS Landranger series 162 Gloucester and Forest of Dean (GR 620122).

The Forest of Dean is a place of natural beauty which offers not just a profusion of walks but camping and caravanning sites, fishing, horse-riding and cycling facilities. There are also opportunities for caving, canoeing and mountain biking. This area has been woodland since ancient times and was certainly exploited by the Romans, was a Royal hunting forest for the Normans, and source of timber for our fighting ships. Today the forest park covers an area of some 35 square miles.

The Walk

From the front entrance of the Speech House turn right and walk for 500 yards to Speech House Woodland which is on the left with a car park, toilets and barbecues. The Speech House oaks are a SSSI (Site of Special Scientific Interest) and were planted in 1808. Hereabouts some woodland was enclosed and wood-burning industries such as iron smelting flourished, but the squatters were evicted by the Court. It was not until after 1750 that encroachment began again.

At the toilets turn left and follow the blue waymarked track through holly, oak and beech woods then half-left along a pathway. The Speech House is now over to your left but a few yards to the right are the Edward VII yews, planted in 1902 to commemorate his coronation. Take the gate ahead and then turn right. In about 100

11

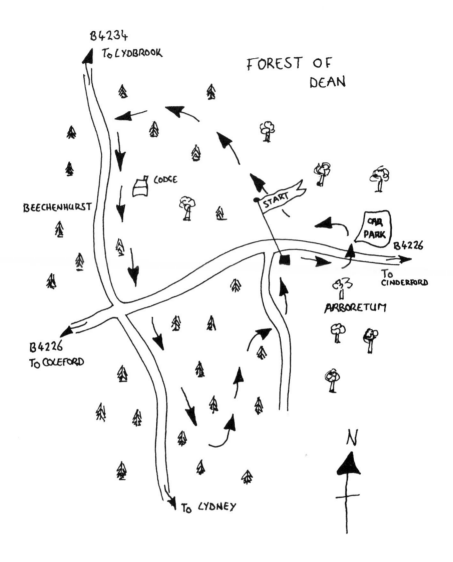

yards a yellow waymark will direct you to the left down a broad track, over a stream then gently uphill into woodland with conifers on the left and beech trees on the right. Walk over a crossing of tracks and slightly to the left you will see the Giant's Chair which is well worth a short detour to admire the excellent view across the forest which it affords. Walk ahead downhill for about 250 yards and turn left at the track junction, now gently downhill, through a gate and into

Beechenhurst Lodge. Here you can obtain refreshments all the year round and shop for forest gifts and guides. There are picnic tables, barbecues, children's adventure playgrounds and flat areas for ball games. It is also the starting point for the famous Sculpture Trail of which the Giant's Chair was just one part.

From Beechenhurst walk ahead in the same general direction, passing through a gate and cattle grid with a green waymark on the left. You walk down a bank and over the B4226, entering Russells Inclosure by the gate opposite. The name of the inclosure is ancient and this area of the forest was first recorded as Russells in 1282 when it appears as Russellum, named after Vivian de Russelhalle, a woodward in the forest in 1270.

Take the broad track ahead which runs gently uphill through conifers with distant views over to the right through timber clearings. The track goes ahead but curves to the left then passes over a stream. As you are walking gently uphill keep an eye and ear open for the raucous sound of the jay in the woodland or circling buzzards overhead.

In this inclosure trees at intersections are carefully numbered, so, armed with the Forestry Commission map of Russells Inclosure, you will know exactly where you are. When you see trees in compartment number 524, turn left on a track which runs uphill to the next junction of tracks some distance away. Here you will find a level track to the left between compartments 524 and 519. Foxgloves are abundant hereabouts in spring as the track goes ahead through conifers then curves to the right and goes very gently uphill.

At the next junction take the track on the right between compartments 520 and 519. This area to the right is called Blackpennywell Green and you are walking between Norway spruce, beech and European larch. In due course you come to Dean Hall School on the left and emerge from this part of the forest through a gate and stile on to a road. Cross the road and enter the forest on the opposite side. After about 25 yards turn left and parallel with the road on greensward within the open forest. As you continue there will be signs indicating the entrance to Speech House Arboretum on the right which you should enter, taking the left path inside the gateway. The trees are all marked by name, date of planting and country of origin. The path bears round to the left and presently you leave the arboretum by way of a gate on the left. Turn half right towards the road, which you then cross and re-enter the car park at Speech House Woodland, or return to the left of the Speech House if you have left your vehicle there.

② Brierley
The Swan Inn

This pleasant roadside inn lies on the northern side of the Forest of Dean in the small settlement of Brierley. It consists of two cosy bars with a good variety of beers and a wide range of bar food.

The draught beers include Castle Eden Ale, Worthington Best Bitter, Murphy's Irish Stout, and Guinness. Heineken, Stella Artois, Labatt's Canadian Lager and Dry Blackthorn cider are also on offer. Bottled beers include Newquay Bitter and Lager, Beck's, Holsten Pils, Kallenburg Pils and Brody. Kaliber is also available.

Main course food falls into three groups. There are snacks, some quite substantial, bar meals and hot pots with, of course, a variety of sweets and ices to follow. The snacks include soup, pies and pasties, toasted sandwiches and many varieties of cold sandwich and bread rolls: you can have doorsteps with the filling to form a ploughman's lunch if you so choose. The bar meals include all the pub favourites such as sirloin steak, gammon steak, chilli con carne, cottage pie, a range of salads, cold ham, egg and chips, Cornish pasty and lasagne. The hot pots include beef curry, chicken curry, sweet and sour pork, vegetable lasagne and beef stew – just right after a bracing walk. The coffee here is excellent, freshly made, attractively served with mints

and brown lump sugar, and very reasonably priced. The Swan Inn is open from 11 am to 4 pm and 6.30 pm to 11 pm, Sunday opening is 12.30 pm to 3 pm and 7 pm to 10.30 pm but lunchtime food is served from 12.30 pm to 2.30 pm.
Telephone: Dean (0594) 860460.

How to get there: The Swan Inn is on the northern side of the A4136 some 3 miles west of Mitcheldean and 9 miles east of Monmouth.

Parking: There is a small car park in front of the inn. There is some possible parking space along the road from the right of the inn in Brierley Banks.

Length of the walk: 3 miles. Map: OS Landranger series 162 Gloucester and Forest of Dean (GR 625152).

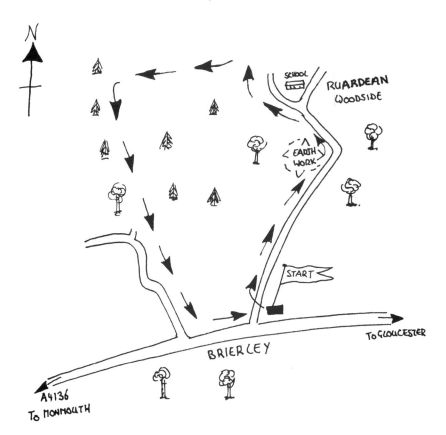

This walk is on the northern extremity of the Forest of Dean and includes quite steeply undulating countryside, entirely wooded, between Upper Lydbrook and Ruardean Woodside. A series of streams crosses the walk in sharp-sided valleys: the music of their rapid flow merges with the woodland birdsong and takes one's mind away from the cares of daily life. North of the walk it is possible to view several grassed-over spoil heaps, a residual of former open-cast coal-mining.

The Walk

From the Swan Inn turn right and right again up the steep slope of Brierley Banks. You will pass extensive oak woods on the left and a series of cottages on the right. The Congregational chapel of 1884 is now the United Reformed Church. It is possible to walk to Ruardean Woodside through the woodland to the left but some of the paths are quite arbitrary and totally unwaymarked. If you attempt that route you will require sound map reading skills and need to be prepared for some steep scrambles up muddy slopes. The straightforward walk is to follow the road ahead through the woodland. In ½ mile it bears sharply left round an earthwork hidden in deep woodland. Just short of Ruardean School take the left road to Newham Bottom which skirts the woodland on the left and playing fields of Ruardean School on the right. In 250 yards take the track which goes ahead and the road bears right. The slope becomes steeply downhill to the left, but in some 200 yards take the path to the right and walk ahead to rejoin the lane on the right.

There is a deep valley ahead and to the left and a view of old coal tip heaps beyond. A solitary waymark on the left of the road is the only guidance you will get on this walk but you should walk down the steep slope then turn off the road sharply to the left down a rough track to the cottages on the hillside. At the last cottage walk steeply ahead to the stream in the distance which is crossed by a narrow footbridge. You should now turn left and left again along a track through the woodland, following the rapidly flowing stream on the left gently downhill in a steep V-shaped valley. Look out or listen for the call of jays in the woodland hereabouts: the cackle is quite distinctive and will echo through the surrounding valley.

In due course a track appears on the opposite side of the stream, then both tracks merge in a Y. Walk ahead with the stream still on your left. At the foot of the slope the track exits to a winding road and you should turn left and follow the road gently uphill with another larger stream on the left flowing fast through a valley of bracken and oak woods in the opposite direction to your line of walk. You will emerge from the woodland on to the A4136 Gloucester to Monmouth road. Turn left along it and into Brierley. The Swan Inn is 50 yards away on the left in High Street.

16

Newent
The George Hotel

This old coaching and posting house dates from 1649 and stands close to the centre of Newent, nearly opposite the fine parish church and the Shambles, which houses the fascinating Museum of Victorian Life. The Courtyard was the former coaching house and is now the restaurant of the hotel.

The George has a bar round three sides of a square forming three separate rooms where drink and bar food may be taken. It is open all day except Sundays, and as a freehouse has a sound selection of beers available. Draught beers include Stones Bitter, Tennent's Extra, Hancock's Bitter, Bass, Brew XI Best Bitter, Toby Bitter and Worthington Dark (a mild). There is also draught Miller Pilsner, Carling Black Label and Guinness. Ciders include Gold Label West Country cider and Strongbow. There is a full series of bottled beers, soft drinks, spirits, and low-alcohol lagers which include John Smith's LA Bitter and Strongbow LA cider. Tea and coffee are served throughout the day.

The food is varied and wholesome, and can be taken either in the bar or in the Courtyard restaurant. There is ample choice and bar meals include four types of omelette, sandwiches with six fillings, six

17

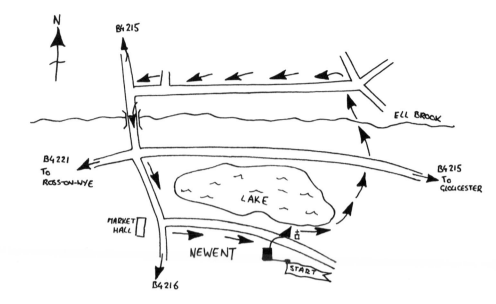

types of ploughman's platter, and jacket potato with six fillings. You can also order steaks, gammon, mixed grill, lasagne, vegetarian lasagne, home-made chilli con carne, curry, chicken tikka masala and a range of salads. The sweets sound delicious, with chocolate nut sundae, hot Belgian apple tart and banana split, among others, on offer. Meals are served from noon to 3 pm, and 7 pm to 10 pm seven days a week. The George also has some ten rooms available on a bed and breakfast basis.

It is worthy of note that when alterations were in progress, a treasure trove of golden spade guineas dated between 1768 and 1798 was found underneath the hearth of the western fireplace in the lounge bar.

Telephone: Newent (0531) 820203.

How to get there: Newent is at the junction of the B4215, B4216 and B4221. Gloucester is 9 miles south-east and Ross-on-Wye some 9 miles west. Junction 3 of the M50 is 3½ miles west of Newent. The George is situated in Church Street, just off Newent High Street.

Parking: There is a car park at the rear of the George Hotel, approached through the archway. There is also on-street parking in the neighbourhood and free car parks just away from the town centre.

Length of the walk: 2 miles. Map: OS Landranger series 162 Gloucester and Forest of Dean (GR 723259).

The walk offers the chance to explore some of the countryside immediately to the north of Newent. To begin with it passes by the church, with a fine nave roof built by Edward Taylor, one of Christopher Wren's carpenters, and passes round Newent lake then over the Ell brook and across fields to Starden. From here the walk can easily be extended to Three Ashes and Oxenhall. The final leg of the walk is along the north of the Ell brook and into Newent at the western end.

The Walk

From the George Hotel turn right and cross the road to the churchyard, passing along the lane to the west of the building. Take the path ahead over the road then turn right in a few yards along the side of Newent lake, which will be on your left. It is home to varieties of duck, moorhen and coot, and is surrounded by stately limes, poplar, sycamore, chestnut and oak trees. You walk round the lake and take the path which goes north passing the end of the water. Eschew the footbridge on the left and walk ahead then round to the left and over a further footbridge. This track leads into the corner of the woodland, with perhaps some difficulty, where there is a way out to cross the bypass. Exactly opposite is a kissing-gate giving access to a further footpath which crosses over a flat meadow. Take the bridge over the stream, which is part of the Ell brook, go through a kissing-gate and in 50 yards cross the main stream by another bridge. The path is quite clear ahead up the slope and over deep pasture towards houses at the top of the rise, You exit from the field by another kissing-gate and turn left along the road side; there is a good grass verge for the most part of this section of the walk on the left. In due course, turn left at the next road junction and in a few hundred yards cross the bypass and enter Newent High Street. You pass the library and the fine west-end of the United Reform Church on the right of the street. At the spectacular timber market hall of Tudor date, standing on 16 oak pillars, turn left into Church Street and return to the George.

⁴ Arlingham
The Red Lion

Arlingham is a substantial village completely enclosed on three sides by a massive loop of the river Severn. The isolation of the village has enabled it to retain some of its old-world charm. It has a dominant church with a tower visible for some miles around and the mass of rich 18th and 19th century memorials in the churchyard give some indication of the wealth the droving trade brought to the locality.

This freehouse serves John Smith's beer and is prominently placed at the central crossroads on the High Street of Arlingham. It is quite clearly a village and an inn which has seen greater days for it was on the road from Arlingham Passage, a mile away, to the west out towards Stroud and the Golden Valley up through the Cotswold escarpment to the east. Arlingham Passage was one of those ferry routes across the river Severn, which in the 18th century and before, brought droves of cattle from their raising grounds in mid and south Wales to the drove roads of England to be transported on the hoof to such places as Banbury and Smithfield market in London.

The Red Lion was the first inn to be found on the eastern side of the Severn over from Newnham. Clearly the inn and the village made considerable income from offering overnight stances for the cattle and sheep in the streets and fields hereabouts, and for the drivers and drovers at the inn itself.

The Red Lion serves four regular cask ales, namely Uley Bitter, Bass, Hook Norton Bitter and the John Smith's range of beers, ample bottled beers and soft drinks along with low-alcohol lagers. Food served ranges from hot and cold snacks to a full à la carte evening menu. There is a special roast meal on Sunday lunchtimes. You can buy sustaining beef sandwiches, ploughman's lunches, chicken or sausage sandwiches or rolls, fish meals or basket meals, such as scampi, every lunchtime. There is a vegetarian selection of vegetable lasagne, pasta and tuna, to be followed by a wide range of puddings. The coffee is excellent. Walkers are welcome to use the inn car park, but there is plenty of space in the wide streets of Arlingham near the inn, and you are asked to make a prior arrangement with the inn if the party is at all large: a complimentary coffee will be served when you give your order. The inn provides a garden and has facilities for skittles, cards, dominoes and shove halfpenny.

Telephone: Gloucester (0452) 740269.

How to get there: From the A38 or M5 (junction 12) take the B4071 which in 4½ miles leads west to Arlingham.

Parking: There is an inn car park and ample space in the village nearby.

Length of the walk: 4½ miles. Map: OS Landranger series 162 Gloucester and Forest of Dean (GR 708109).

The axis of the village is broadly north-south and there are houses and farms spread out amid orchards and paddocks without much of the infilling one sees elsewhere in the county. The quiet roads and lanes hereabouts are a haven for weekend cyclists and walkers. It is in easy and flat walking country but with a full measure of interest and variety of scenery and riverine wildlife.

The Walk
From the Red Lion turn right past the village store. The village hall is on the right with the old school on the left, founded in 1768 and endowed by the John Yate Charity. Further along the street is St Augustine's working farm which can be visited if time and schedules permit. At the junction by Slowwe Cottages take the waymarked track which runs ahead. The track bends round Warth Cottage with old orchards to left and right. You may see the odd heron in this area or hear the sound of woodpeckers pecking furiously at trees. Garden birds abound: thrushes, blackbirds, the flash of a wren or in the

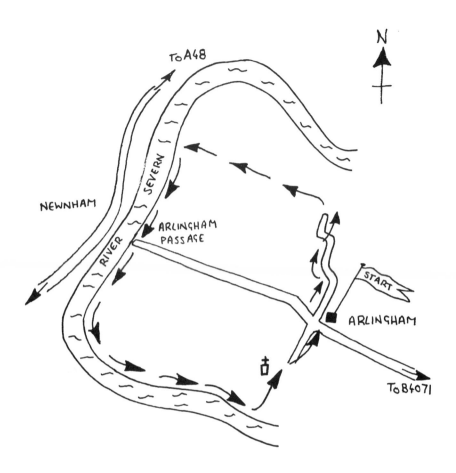

distance a flock of lapwings flying up from a damp pasture.

The track takes several right-angled corners and in due course comes to a junction by oak trees. Walk on the track ahead to a pair of gates some 150 yards away: take the right-hand gate into a field with the ditch kept to the left. There are no waymarks but walk round the field edge, keeping it to the left. Over to the right is a reed bed, the home of swans and duck, while the fields abound in larks. Two stiles appear on the left, which you cross, then turn right, keeping the unwaymarked course with the field boundary on the right. Cross the right-hand gate at the end of the pasture and walk ahead along a grass track beside ploughland. You cross a gate and mount the embankment and turn left along the side of the Severn, with a deep ditch on the left. Over on the opposite bank is the busy A48 running into Newnham.

Crossing stiles and gates ahead, you come to Arlingham Passage with the Old Passage Inn on the left at the point where the ferry crossing from Newnham landed on the eastern side of the Severn. Continue along the embankment, part of the Severn Way Path, crossing a succession of stiles and gates. You will see a boatyard on the opposite bank and may observe countless sea birds, water fowl, curlew, snipe and peewits.

Just short of the twin pylons and electricity cables turn left over a sluice and along a waymarked track. There is another deep drainage ditch to the right which presently veers off to the right and is replaced by old orchards on the right. You pass a cottage, The Folly, on the left, then farm buildings and a pair of cottages. The track swings round to the right and left with old orchards, some trees having great clumps of mistletoe, to left and right. Arlingham church tower is now clearly in view and the churchyard is well worth inspection, as is the one-handed clock in the tower. You walk ahead amid the generally well spaced houses back to the crossroads at the centre of the village, on which the Red Lion lies.

⑤ Stone
The Berkeley Vale Inn

The Berkeley Vale Inn is a large and imposing hostelry standing beside the A38 in the centre of the small village of Stone. Being about halfway between Bristol and Gloucester on this former turnpike road, the Berkeley Vale Inn clearly serviced the horse-drawn coaches, wagons and carriages of an earlier era. Indeed the inn maintained an importance well into the second half of this century by being sited so strategically on one of the major routes through Gloucestershire. The building of the M5, barely a mile to the east, ended all this: the inn retains it structural prominence but the high volume passing trade is now contained by the neighbouring motorway.

Consequently the inn is now a freehouse and serves a range of draught beer, cider and soft drinks in the bar, which has a wood-burning fire. Off at one end of the bar is a large games room with pool, darts, skittles, a juke-box, electronic games and satellite TV. At the other end of the bar is the large dining-room and restaurant. Bar food can also be eaten in the bar.

Draught beer includes Tetley Bitter and Smiles Best Bitter, the latter brewed in Bristol. There is Carlsberg lager, Dry Blackthorn cider and Merrydown cider all on draught with several non- or low-alcohol lagers. There is a beer garden at the rear.

Food is divisible into bar food and restaurant food. From the bar menu you may choose between jacket potato, pizza, toasties, sandwiches, sausage, egg and chips and a series of ploughman's lunches. From the restaurant menu you may order such dishes as sirloin steak, roast chicken, cannelloni, beef curry and rice, trout, scampi, nut roast, vegetable crumble, omelette and various salads and sweets. There is a special traditional roast on Sundays which may be taken by prior booking only. The inn has accommodation. Telephone: Thornbury (0454) 260219.

How to get there: Stone is some 15 miles north-east of Bristol at the boundary with Avon. Take the A38 from the Gloucester direction and the B4066/A38 from Dursley. The village is a mile north of junction 14 on the M5.

Parking: There is ample parking at the Berkeley Vale Inn. You may also be able to park off the A38 beside the village green.

Length of the walk: 3 miles and 4 miles. Map: OS Landranger series 162 Gloucester and Forest of Dean (GR 684955).

Stone is a typical small village in this part of the Vale of Berkeley, wedged between the Severn estuary and the escarpment of the Cotswold Hills. In rolling and stony countryside straddling the little river Avon (Berkeley Pill) it has a large village green, several Georgian houses beside the main road and a church on the green whose 15th century spire can be seen for miles around. Inside, the east window is in memory of the Revd. Charles Cripps who was incumbent here for nearly 50 years.

The Walk

From the Berkeley Vale Inn cross the A38 and head left of the village church for the green, which you cross. Beyond the church take the lane and walk ahead, passing Court Mead on the left. Walk on down the lane but at the gate to Westend House turn left on to the waymarked bridleway. This becomes a very well defined lane bordered by hedges, pastures and oak trees undulating gently across this portion of the Vale of Berkeley. At some times of the year parts of the track can be deep in water and mud, so go prepared. You cross the stream by a wide bridge and in a short distance emerge on to a road.

From here you may extend the walk by a mile, by continuing along the bridleway to Appleridge Farm at Hystfield then returning by the neighbouring bridleway to Lower Stone which gives an extended walk of 4 miles. Alternatively, for the 3 mile walk, turn left along the

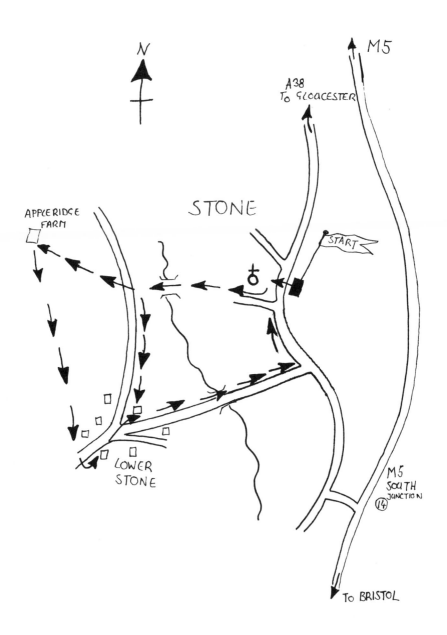

N

M5

A38
TO GLOUCESTER

STONE

START

APPLERIDGE
FARM

LOWER
STONE

M5
SOUTH
JUNCTION
(14)

TO BRISTOL

road, passing left and right a series of isolated farms and cottages such as Holly Tree Lodge and Lower Stone Farm. This is a countryside of ash, willow, holly and oak trees, here scattered along field boundaries, there placed in copse and woodland, dividing up the beef pastures and horse paddocks.

In due course you cross a stream near Lower Stone Farm and a footpath waymarked to the left will take you directly back to Stone across the fields if you so wish. However, the walk continues ahead along the road, passing Manor Farm on the left with a pond on the right into Lower Stone, a village of red stone houses covered by pantiles. Turn left at the road junction by Howard House and shortly left again towards Stone, with an extensive orchard on the left and copse on the right. The Glebe and the Yews are left and right along the road and further on an old stone bridge crosses over a stream as Stone church spire comes into good view a mile away across the fields. Passing Stone District Survey Laboratories of Nuclear Electric on the left, you enter the village at Court Mead. Just past Stone village hall turn left along the A38 and beyond Court Moat on the right is the Berkeley Vale Inn where you may have to clear your boots of the distinctive local red mud.

North Nibley
The Black Horse Inn

This inn dominates the centre of North Nibley and comprises one of the oldest domestic buildings in the village, indeed it may have been a coaching inn in its time on the Wotton-under-Edge to Berkeley road. Inside the low ceilinged timbered inn there is a dining-room at either end (one non-smoking) and a substantial bar which is both long and timbered in the centre part of the building. A couple of large open hearth fires blaze a welcoming heat in winter.

Draught beers served include Flowers BB, Boddingtons Bitter, Flowers Original strong ale, Brakspear's Bitter (of Henley-on-Thames) and Cooper's Wickwar Pale Ale. There are also Guinness, Heineken, Stella Artois, Murphy's Irish Stout, Bulmer's Original Cider and Strongbow. In addition the inn serves Kaliber, White Label and Strongbow low alcohol.

The bar menu of this Whitbread inn is available between 12 noon and 2 pm and from 7 pm to 10 pm each day, except Sunday when the evening menu ceases at 9.30 pm. Food and drink may be taken in the dining-rooms and in the bar, where tables and chairs are available. There is also a beer garden at the rear for summer use. Snacks include jacket potatoes with seven possible fillings, ploughman's lunches with

28

four combinations, and sandwiches with seven fillings. There is also home-made soup and pâté and toast. The specialities include breast of chicken, beef, mushroom and Guinness pie, lamb goulash, Madras beef curry, home-made lasagne and chilli con carne. Vegetarian dishes include vegetable tikka masala and vegetable Mexicana.

You may order grilled rump steak, grilled gammon steak or Cajun chicken breast. The à la carte meals may be taken in one of the dining-rooms and include such items as poached salmon, tuna steak, grilled trout and beef Stroganov. The sweets are delicious and include hot chocolate fudge cake, steamed treacle sponge pudding and apple pie. There is an extensive wine list. Accommodation is available to the extent of six rooms, four of them en suite, and one family room. The inn has quiet music, no juke-box and no fruit machines, but you may play darts and dominoes.

Telephone: Dursley (0453) 546841.

How to get there: North Nibley is on the B4060, 2 miles north-west of Wotton-under-Edge and 3½ miles from the junction with the A38 at Berkeley Road. The Black Horse Inn is at the crossroads in the centre of the village.

Parking: There is a small car park on the opposite side of the road from the inn and a small parking bay in front of the Black Horse. There is also space to park off the main road beyond the inn.

Length of the walk: 2 miles. Map: OS Landranger series 162 Gloucester and Forest of Dean (GR 741958).

Although this would appear to be a short walk it is in fact very strenuous and steep. It follows part of the Cotswold Way and can consequently be added to at will. It makes a good summer afternoon walk with a picnic at the monument on Nibley Knoll. The Tyndale Monument is to commemorate the local martyr William Tyndale and is a dominating landmark hereabouts. A notice at the foot of the path indicates that the Tyndale Monument can be ascended for a small charge; with two addresses to obtain the key.

The Walk

From the Black Horse Inn walk along the main road towards Wotton-under-Edge. In 100 yards turn left along the waymarked Cotswold Way up a well maintained but steeply rising track in a ravine through holly and beech woods. Near the top of the hill, short of a gate across the route, turn right on a waymarked footpath: the path curves round to the right. Cross a stile and leave the wood to emerge on to the flat, grassy top of the limestone cap. From here there are far-ranging views.

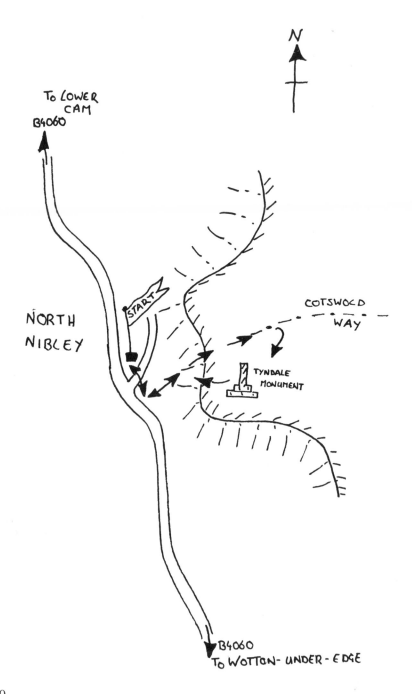

N

To LOWER
CAM
B4060

NORTH
NIBLEY

START

COTSWOLD
WAY

TYNDALE
MONUMENT

B4060
TO WOTTON-UNDER-EDGE

A topograph erected to commemorate the Queen's Silver Jubilee in 1977 indicates that the Sugar Loaf in the Brecon Beacons is 33 miles, Severn Bridge 12 miles, Lansdown above Bath 17 miles and Berkeley 4 miles. The view along the Cotswold edge is truly magnificent, so too the view up and down the Severn estuary and into the hills of central Wales, Exmoor, the Quantocks and Severnside.

The monument lies towards the edge from the topograph and is enclosed in an ornate metal pen. It is suitably inscribed to William Tyndale, translator of the English Bible, who caused the New Testament to be published in English. Born nearby, possibly at Hunts Court Farm, he was martyred at Vilvorde, Flanders, on 6th October 1536. It is 111 ft high and set 700 ft up on the Cotswold escarpment on the route of the Cotswold Way. The Tyndale Monument was erected through public subscription in 1866.

The path down from the monument is just past and to the right of the memorial. Take the path to the right over a stile and into the woods. It is another well maintained path which descends the very steep slope in a series of steps through the shelter of the woods, nevertheless the distant roar of traffic on the M5 is ever present. Especially in wet weather, water issuing from the limestone and underlying strata can make this path extremely muddy. In due course the steps end and the path rejoins the Cotswold Way. Walk downhill to the Wotton-under-Edge road then turn right along it to return to the Black Horse Inn.

An interesting further facet of North Nibley's history is that what may have been the last private battle between rival barons took place here when William, Lord Berkeley and Viscount De Lisle fought it out in 1471.

Epney
The Anchor

This pub is ideally located beside the river Severn on the outside of a large meander of the river just below Longney Crib. From the garden and terrace of the inn a consequent extensive view can be had both up and downstream. This is apparently a good place for elvers and to catch a view of the famous Severn Bore.

The Anchor has two extensive bars and the picture windows of the lounge give sheltered views along the river. Draught beers on tap include Castle Eden Ale, Flowers Best Bitter, Bass, Boddingtons Bitter, West Country Traditional Pale Ale, Moosehead Ale – a Canadian export, Murphy's Irish Stout, and Guinness. Heineken and Stella Artois are also on offer. There is Gold Label cider, West Country cider, Stowford Press Traditional Dry cider and Weston's Much Marcle cider. Low-alcohol lagers are also available.

Food on offer comprises a mixture of daily specials, bar snacks, main courses and sweets. Such fare as faggots, peas and chips, steak pie or beef curry make up the daily specials which naturally change from time to time. Basket meals with children's portions, jacket potatoes with five different fillings, five varieties of sandwiches and

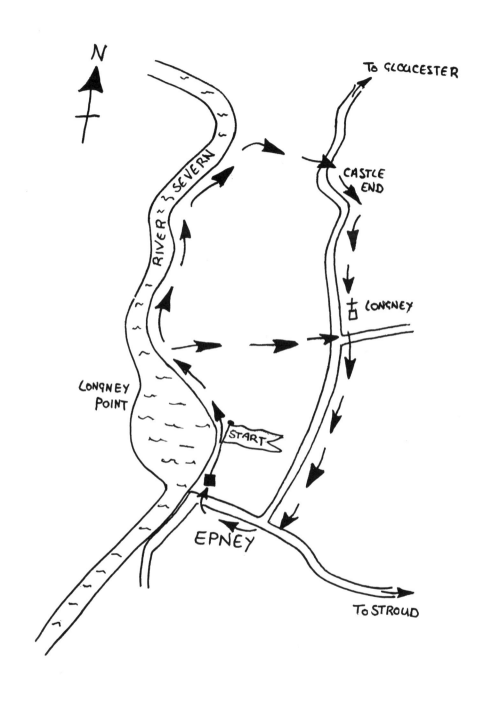

N

TO GLOUCESTER

CASTLE END

LONGNEY

RIVER SEVERN

LONGNEY POINT

START

EPNEY

TO STROUD

rolls, ploughman's lunches of Cheddar, Stilton or ham comprise the snacks.

The main menu has starters such as soup, whitebait or Japanese style prawns with main courses chosen from such items as rump steak, gammon, chicken, scampi and home-made steak and Guinness pie. The inn also offers entertainment in the form of darts and shove-halfpenny and has the longest skittle alley in Gloucestershire. Telephone: Gloucester (0452) 740433.

How to get there: Turn off the A38 just over a mile south of its junction with the B4008, which is very close to junction 12 of the M5. Epney is 2 miles west on the minor road over the Gloucester and Sharpness canal.

Parking: There is a large car park at the side of the inn with some space in the road nearby.

Length of the walk: 5 miles. Map: OS Landranger series 162 Gloucester and Forest of Dean (GR 762110).

Epney is a compact village hemmed in by the river Severn on the west and surrounded by orchards and meadows on the other three sides. A mile away is the highly active Gloucester and Sharpness canal and the direct route out of the village to the A38 crosses a busy swingbridge over the canal. One of the main attractions of the village is its juxtaposition with a scenic loop of the river Severn.

The Walk

From the inn turn right along the Severn Way over a footbridge and sluice which takes you through orchard land and passes a series of isolated cottages on the right down below the defensive river embankment. At Longney Crib the river narrows, then at Longney Point upstream it widens into a large pool, mostly mud-filled at low tide. The path follows the side of the river, under pylons in due course, for just over ½ mile. This is a good area to view the sea and water birds which abound on this part of the Severn.

After a while you will pass beside a corner of woodland, then at the northern end turn right along a footpath which leads east away from the river towards Castle End. It may be muddy here over ploughed fields and some grassland, but at certain times of year it is a good spot to view flocks of lapwing.

At Castle End turn right along the minor road which winds through both pasture and plough-land then extensive orchards into Longney. You pass the school on the right and the trim church of St Laurence on the left. There is a large wayside pond on the south side of the

34

church. At Manor Farm, just beyond the pond, turn right towards Epney, passing Lynch Farm on the left.

You enter Epney by Willow Cottage on the left and orchard land on the right which leads over to the embankment beside the river. At the telephone box turn right and in 250 yards you will be back at the Anchor car park.

8 Coaley
The Fox and Hounds

The Fox and Hounds is a bright and well maintained freehouse at which you will get a warm welcome. It is the only inn in the neighbourhood and now the only retail business in Coaley. The inn has low ceilings with timbers, two bars and a dining-room but also a dining area in the bar. Outside is a skittle alley: inside you may play darts.

The draught beers on offer are both interesting and wide-ranging. There is Boddingtons Bitter, Foxley Bitter, Flowers Best Bitter, Whitbread Poacher's Bitter, Uley Bitter and Mole's Best Bitter. You may also have Stella Artois, Heineken and low-alcohol lagers.

The Fox and Hounds serves food between noon and 2 pm each day, except Monday, and between 7 pm and 9 pm on Friday, Saturday and Sunday. The bar menu contains all the old favourites including tasty ham and cheese rolls. You can have plaice or cod and chips, chicken Kiev, chicken cordon bleu, chicken and mushroom pie and chicken tikka masala, also beef and ale pie, moussaka, beef korma and cottage pie. Vegetarians can have omelettes or vegetable curry. Also on the menu is chilli con carne, lasagne verde and gammon steaks.

Telephone: Dursley (0453) 890366.

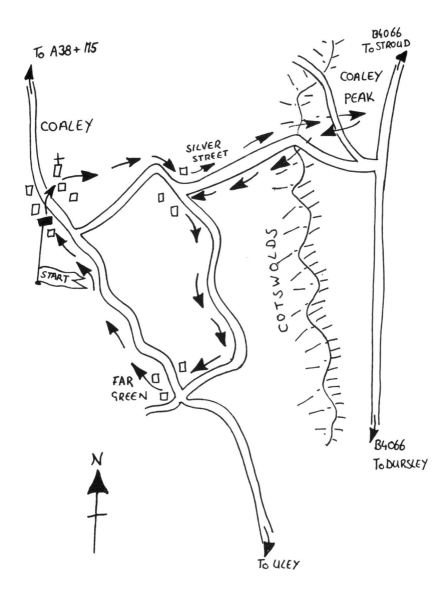

How to get there: Coaley is located broadly equidistant from junctions on the B4066 at Coaley Peak, the A4135 near Lower Cam and the A38 at Cambridge. Junction 13 of the M5 is 5 miles to the north. The Fox and Hounds is near the centre of this straggling village, quite close to the church.

37

Parking: There is a car park at the Fox and Hounds or you can find parking near the church.

Length of the walk: 3 miles, or 5 miles if you take the extension to the top of the Cotswolds at Coaley Peak. Map: OS Landranger series 162 Gloucester and Forest of Dean (GR 772015).

This walk falls into two parts. There is a 3 mile circuit which can be completed on the flat starting at Coaley or a 5 mile walk which takes in Coaley Peak. This addition to the walk is pretty but arduous for some of the gradients are steep and part of the walking is rough. As an alternative it is possible to park in the extensive car park on Coaley Peak, take in the splendid panorama from the top of the Cotswolds, then walk down to Coaley for lunch and return to Coaley Peak by way of Far Green, unless you can arrange for one of your party to drive down to Coaley to meet you there, in which case the walk is downhill all the way.

The Walk

From the Fox and Hounds turn left along the road towards the church. On the right you will find a footpath just short of the church which heads off to Silver Street. Follow this path across the fields for just over ½ mile until it leads you into the road junction at Silver Street. Follow the road ahead for several hundred yards then take Peak Lane on the left. This narrow and quiet road is increasingly steep and leads up in just over a mile to the National Trust land below and around Coaley Peak. Near the National Trust sign on the left is a path up the gradient which will be a scramble through undergrowth to Coaley Peak picnic site. From here the views are extensive both up and down the Severn estuary and over to the south and mid-Wales mountains.

Return the way you have come and walk down Peak Lane through the woodland either side of the road and passing Upper Silver Street Farm where you turn left along the road which winds round to the Ham. Here you follow the road to the right for ½ mile to the crossroads where you turn right through the hamlets of Far Green and Hamshill and return to the Fox and Hounds.

If you have the chance, take a look inside Coaley church. The 14th century tower is the only remaining part of the old church, for the building was burnt down. There is a fine modern stained glass window commemorating Richard Caddy who was for 44 years schoolmaster, choirmaster and organist in Coaley, while in the chancel is the memorial brass of the 16th century to Daniel Stayn. Portrayed in a long cloak and ruff he is shown with his three children kneeling with his wife, who is typically clothed in a long dress and veil.

Ashleworth Quay
The Boat Inn

The Boat Inn, which is situated right on the river Severn above Gloucester, is one of those delightful old-world pubs which one rarely finds nowadays, located in an idyllic riverine setting. The main theme of this pub, with its single small bar, is conversation, ably initiated and fostered by the two ladies who preside over the welcoming and friendly freehouse. The locals are both interesting and interested in visitors: one is made to feel welcome and is guided into the conversation which ebbs and flows around the bar. Off from the bar is a small room for drinking and eating, warmed by an old-style kitchen range and having larger tables for parties to sit round. In the yard outside is a shelter for eating and drinking next to the small garden: ideal for use in summer months.

Of the beers and ciders on tap note ought to be made of Smiles Best Bitter, Arkell's 3B, Yeoman and Flowers Best Bitter. There is Stowford Press cider, Exmoor Gold, and Heineken and Carlsberg Export lagers, along with a range of low-alcohol lagers. The coffee is excellent, and you can have a game of dominoes if there should be a lull in the conversation.

The food is refreshingly simple, wholesome and freshly home-

39

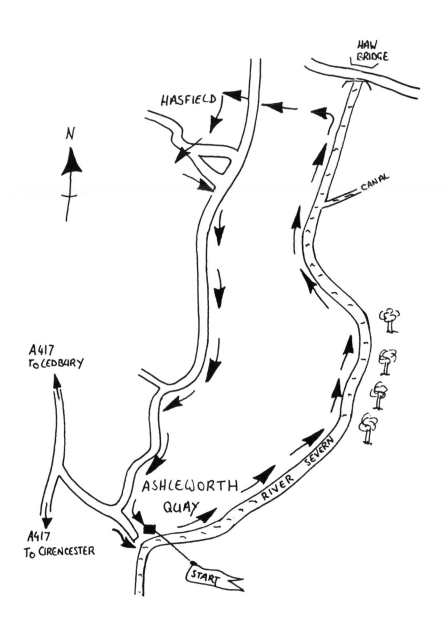

HAW BRIDGE

HASFIELD

N

CANAL

A417 TO LEDBURY

RIVER SEVERN

ASHLEWORTH QUAY

A417 TO CIRENCESTER

START

made. It consists of white or brown rolls or baps liberally filled with ham or cheese, salad and pickle. You can also buy substantial ploughman's lunches. What else could a hungry walker ask for? If at all possible it would be a good idea for parties of walkers to ring ahead to let the proprietors know they are coming so that suitable arrangements can be made.

Telephone: Gloucester (0452) 700272.

How to get there: Ashleworth is off the A417 Gloucester to Ledbury road. From Gloucester, turn right at Hartpury which is about 5 miles from Gloucester. Take the road indicated to Ashleworth and, beyond the tithe barn and church, the Boat Inn is at the end of the lane which leads to the river.

Parking: There is a small car park at the inn. It may also be possible to find limited parking space in Ashleworth.

Length of the walk: 7 miles. Map: OS Landranger series 162 Gloucester and Forest of Dean (GR 819251).

Ashleworth Quay lies on a superb part of the river Severn and this fairly long walk takes in a variety of countryside, some of which you may find muddy at particular times of the year. Ashleworth itself has two fine 15th century houses which can be viewed by advance arrangement and a tithe barn of the same era, in the care of the National Trust.

The Walk

From the car park of the Boat Inn turn left along the side of the river Severn and walk upstream along the Severn Way path. This is a straightforward walk to Haw Bridge and the route is well marked and gently curves round Basfield Ham to take on a northerly direction. The views up and down and over the river are of great beauty. On the opposite side the steeply rising land of Sandhurst Hill falls down to the river bank which in due course becomes heavily wooded for nearly a mile. Birdlife abounds: a keen ear is often more important than a keen eye on this stretch of the river to identify the various species.

At the end of the wood the path curves left as the river loops. Opposite, past the Cliff, the river Chelt enters the Severn near a picturesque inn and in a short distance is the river junction of the disused Coomb Hill canal which led from the Severn to carry goods up to the Gloucester to Tewkesbury road nearly 3 miles away.

From here onwards the path swings gently left and then right again, with a small wood on your left. In about a mile you pass buildings including Haw Farm and see the B4213 and Haw Bridge ahead.

Short of the bridge and inn turn left at the waymarked path and bear left at the left corner of the field. You go over the pasture ahead to a further stile by a gate, then turn right over a bridge and over a stile at the next boundary. Walk ahead along the road for some 200 yards then turn left at the second waymark through a garden and orchard. At the end you cross a bridge and follow the field boundary, keeping it on your right until you emerge on to a road. If you cross the road you will find steps up the opposite bank.

Bear round Great House to a gate which is at the far right-hand corner of the meadow. Go ahead over the next field to a stile, keeping Hasfield Court to your right. From here you walk over a further field to a stile at the edge which leads into an orchard. You leave the orchard by the gate to a road. Turn left along the road and at the next junction take the right fork. You will soon come to a further junction where you turn right along the minor road. In about a mile you pass Stonebow Farm and the road curves round to the right. Turn left at the next junction through White End and in a few hundred yards left again to Ashleworth Quay, passing the church and tithe barn on your left.

Ashleworth Tithe Barn is a National Trust property (open April to end October daily 9 am to 6 pm but closed on Good Friday). The barn is 120 ft in length and dates from the 15th century. It has two projecting porch bays and fine roof timbers with queenposts.

Also worth visiting in Ashleworth Quay are two fine houses. Ashleworth Court is a limestone manor house of the 15th century with splendid roof timbers in the great hall. Telephone: 0452 70350. Ashleworth Manor is another 15th century house which is timber-framed and has interesting carved ceiling beams. Telephone: 0452 70241.

Longford
The Globe Inn

10

This freehouse is warm and cosy inside – with one bar, a substantial area for bar snacks and an adjacent dining room. Outside, there is a large garden and children's play area, beside the river Severn. The range of beer on offer is also good with draught Hanson's Bitter, Banks's Bitter, John Smith's Bitter, Flowers Bitter and Camerons' Strongarm. Also on offer are such lagers as Harp, Kronenbourg, Heineken and Fosters. Ciders include Gold Label West Country and Strongbow. There is also draught Guinness and a wide range of bottled soft drinks and lager, together with low-alcohol Kaliber and White Label.

Food comprises both bar snacks and a full menu. You can select from a range of ploughman's lunches, jacket potatoes, sandwiches and pizza, together with sausage, egg and chips. Main courses include scampi, lasagne, a variety of steaks, roast chicken, home-made chicken and mushroom pie. There is a vegetarian menu, a Sunday roast lunch, a variety of mouthwatering sweets, and a good wine list.

Telephone: Gloucester (0452) 414651.

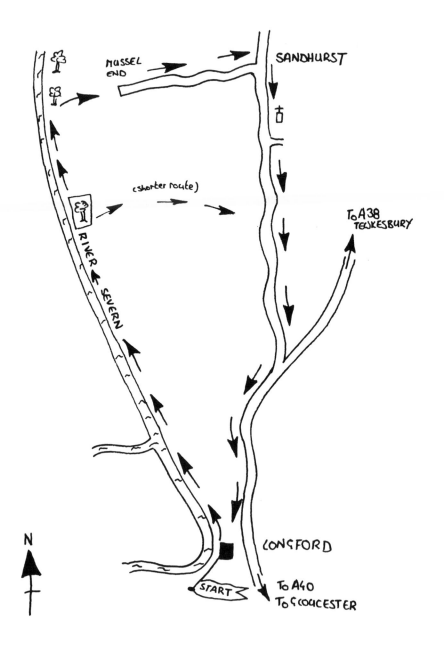

MUSSEL
END

SANDHURST

(shorter route)

RIVER SEVERN

To A38
TEWKESBURY

CONGFORD

N

START

To A40
To GLOUCESTER

How to get there: Longford is 1½ miles north of Gloucester city centre and is best reached from Kingsholm on the minor road which leads to Sandhurst, or from the A38 Tewkesbury to Gloucester road turning off at Twigworth towards Sandhurst and Longford.

Parking: There is a large car park adjacent to the inn; it may also be possible to park beside the road nearby.

Length of the walk: 4½ miles (but can easily be shortened to 3¼ miles). Map: OS Landranger series 162 Gloucester and Forest of Dean (GR 829207).

This riverine walk is along the earliest portion of the non-tidal river Severn, just above Gloucester. Here the river is in all its glory, wide, quite straight and willow fringed with backwaters beside the main stream which form substantial ponds abounding in wildlife and in one place turned into a nature reserve. The walk is largely through knee-deep pasture beside the river which at one time of the year is abundant in buttercups and other wild flowers. The return portion of the walk passes through Sandhurst and along a meandering, quiet, country lane with here and there timber-framed cottages and farms beside the route.

The Walk

From the back door of the inn (which is, in reality, the main entrance), take the small wicket gate a step or so away which lets immediately on to the river Severn towpath. Turn right and walk upstream, the paved path in due course giving way to grass as it runs high above the swiftly-flowing river. Willow, hawthorn, wild roses and hops line the path which in due course turns right and left over a sluice gate to cross a tributary stream before it rejoins the river bank as part of the Severn Way path. It passes between the river and a swampy backwater on the right then over a waymarked footbridge into a meadow passing under power lines. Follow the path ahead along the flood embankment through fields of grazing beef and dairy cattle. A stile takes you into a wood with a waste manufactory on the right, which is quite well shielded from the river. You pass over a stile into a meadow and the waymarked path is parallel with pylons as you pass over a second stile into a further long meadow. Over the river to the left is the white block of Maisemore House set in a park of colourful and ornamental trees, high above the river flood level.

One has all kinds of excitements on many of these walks. One unexpected view in a neighbouring field was, in broad daylight, a mature fox being chased by a herd of bullocks in full cry. I had to get my binoculars out just to check that the bullocks were not being ridden by little men in red coats, and sure enough, they were not!

45

In due course a further stile and gate takes the path into a wood fringed by a backwater which comprises Sandhurst Nature Reserve. If you wish to take the shorter walk turn right here alongside the wood then pass through a gap in the hedge at the corner. Go across the field and under the pylons in the same general direction. Soon a ditch will appear on the left and a prominent oak tree half right. Cross the waymarked gate and walk straight on keeping the field boundary on the right passing just to the right of the isolated farm building. You walk ahead on to a farm track which you follow to its junction with the Sandhurst to Longford road at Gardiner's Farm.

The longer walk continues ahead alongside the Severn and through the Nature Reserve. A little distance ahead, having exited from the reserve, take the footpath which bears off to the right. It passes through orchards and at Mussel End becomes a road leading into Sandhurst. At the junction of roads turn right and pass Sandhurst church on the left. Keep walking down this winding by-road until your reach Gardiner's Farm on the right where the shorter route now joins the walk. This farm house is a delightful thatched and timbered cottage with some slightly incongruous outbuildings and the road back to Longford winds through pasture with isolated cottages in a similar style here and there. At Linden Villa a distant view of Gloucester Cathedral tower comes into view ahead, with Maisemore church tower half-right. At the road junction beside another ancient and timbered cottage, take the road ahead past Abloads Court. In half-a-mile you will be back at the Globe Inn.

⑪ Leighterton
The Royal Oak

'Real Ale, good food, children's room.' This freehouse in the centre of the small village of Leighterton is over 300 years old, wholly stone-built, south-facing with a large tree standing on the western side of the inn. There is a friendly welcome for all visitors and an extensive range of traditional ales including Theakston Old Peculier, Butcombe Bitter, Reverend James and Hook Norton BB. You can also obtain, on draught, Guinness, Foster's lager and Kronenbourg. There are low-alcohol lagers together with non-alcoholic Iceberg.

As if to complement the excellent beer list there is a good food menu which will satisfy the appetite of the most hungry of walkers. The menu is divided into snacks, main course meals, salads and sweets. Side orders are available and there is a children's menu at lunchtime. In addition to the normal menu, traditional Sunday lunch is available.

The snacks include farmhouse soup, country style pâté, deep fried mushrooms, three types of ploughman's lunch, French sticks garnished with salad and filled with Cheddar or ham and spicy bean burger for vegetarians. The main courses include plaice, seafood platter, rump steak, gammon, home-made steak and kidney pie, lasagne, with meat or vegetarian, American fried chicken, West Country pork and Gloucestershire sausages – locally made giant pork sausages served with baked or chipped potatoes and peas or baked beans. Sweets feature home-made Bramley apple pie, butterscotch or chocolate sundae and fresh meringue and whipped cream. A variety of coffees are also available. The children's menu includes cod fish fingers and sausage and chips.

Food is served from noon to 2 pm daily and 7 pm to 10 pm (except Monday evening) but until 9 pm on Sunday. There is a good skittle alley, which is also available for private hire.

Telephone: Tetbury (0666) 890250.

How to get there: Leighterton is just off the A46 Bath to Stroud road and is well signposted. It is some 8 miles south of Stroud and 18 miles north of Bath. The village is about 5 miles west of Tetbury, using a minor road from the A4135.

Parking: There is a large parking area at the side of the inn; please ask if you want to leave your car while you walk, particularly at busy times. There is suitable parking elsewhere in the village, possibly between the inn and the church.

Length of the walk: 4½ miles and 6 miles. Map: OS Landranger series 162 Gloucester and Forest of Dean (GR 823912).

This is two walks within one interesting circuit in this gently undulating part of the Cotswolds. The longer walk goes along the northern side of the Westonbirt Arboretum, which contains one of the world's finest collections of temperate trees and shrubs. It is one of the most colourful places in Gloucestershire, both in the spring at rhododendron time and in autumn when the trees are in full colour. The arboretum is open all the year round, generally from 10 am to 8 pm (with maximum daylight) and is well worth a visit.

The Walk
From the pub turn right then left along the road taking the left fork at the junction and walking past the church. The village is a network of pretty lanes and quite charming old stone cottages, converted barns and pigeon lofts. Walk past the church on the left and Duck House on the right. At the crossroads beyond the duck-pond take the lane on the left towards Knockdown, which runs partly between substantial dry-stone walls and high earthen banks topped with a wall or hedge: this gives much needed shelter on wet or windy days in this exposed part of the Cotswolds. The land runs gently downhill into the welcome of a dry valley. In due course turn left along a waymarked bridleway

48

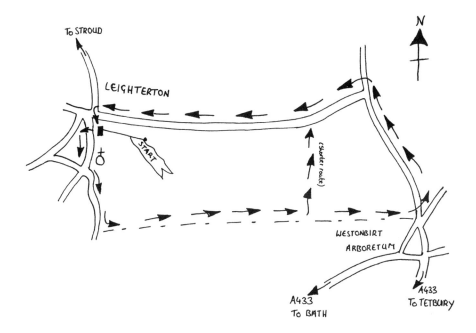

which is a wide and well rutted track running between oak and ash trees, over a series of gates, again falling gently down the slope. Woodland appears ahead and the valley deepens into a more enclosing V-shape.

Go over a gate and into a much broader section of track with woodland ahead to both left and right with a high dry-stone wall on the right. Walk ahead into the wood of silver birch, ash, sycamores, and conifers near the top of the slope. This is at the edge of Westonbirt Arboretum. Watch out for badger setts hereabouts and be ready for extremely muddy conditions in wet weather. Some distance ahead at a crossing of tracks which is regrettably unwaymarked, you have the option of a shorter route. For the longer route move to the next paragraph. *The short walk* turns left along the level of the muddy valley bottom. There is a gate ahead which exits from the wood into pasture with woodland still bordering the left of the walk. There is again no waymark but walk ahead, keeping the field boundary to the left in the constricting V of a limestone valley. Up the slope to the right are remnants of small stone quarries which may have provided materials for the track floor and the walls hereabouts, but they are now quite grassed over. There is a spur of woodland protruding up to the right and pheasant breeding on the left. The track now begins to rise gently and curves to the left up the dry valley. Ahead, cross the fieldgate on

49

to the road and turn left. This route is now joined by the longer walk, for joint directions move on one paragraph.

The longer walk continues ahead, briefly over a pasture and along the northern border of the arboretum for about a mile, then passes through parkland and on to a minor road along which you walk to the left. In a further mile turn left at the crossroads to return to Leighterton.

The lane rises gently up from the dry valley, passing a farmhouse, buildings and waterpump on the left, and in due course the modern buildings of Bennett's Farm on the right. The stumpy spire of Leighterton church is now well in sight ahead.

At the bend in the road at the edge of the village take a walk into the village cemetery, for here you will see the memorials to 23 of the 25 young men of the Australian Flying Corps who were killed in flying accidents during the First World War at what was then a training airfield just north of the village. In the church porch and by the war memorial inside the building is a further list of the dead with full details of their next-of-kin in Australia. So deeply does the village feel about these tragedies that the village British Legion commemorates ANZAC Day in the church. The walk continues into the village and ends at the Royal Oak.

12 Tiltups End
Tipputs Inn

This is a substantial freehouse standing at a junction of lanes and tracks radiating from the inn. Being close to the edge of the Cotswold escarpment it is placed in attractive walking country. Tipputs Inn has a high, timbered, L-shaped bar with tables and chairs at each end for dining. The room is stone- and bare brick-walled in a most pleasing manner. There is an open fire in season and a beer garden for summer use.

The draught beer on offer is wide-ranging in type and provenance. There is Hook Norton's Old Hooky, John Smith's Bitter, Ruddles BB and Smiles Bitter, from Colston Yard in Bristol. There is also draught Guinness and draught Budweiser, Murphy's Irish Stout, Beamish Stout, Foster's lager, Holsten Export with Dry Blackthorn and Autumn Gold cider. You may also buy Hofmeister lager, Clausterhaler, low-alcohol lager and coffee. The bar hours are 11.30 am to 2.30 pm (3 pm on Sundays) and 6.30 pm to 11 pm (7 pm to 10.30 pm on Sundays).

Amid the flower pots, luxurious plants and the pictures around the walls – many of them Victorian theatrical prints – you will find the blackboards which indicate the food menu. They consist of starters and snacks but also chef's specials, which had an Italian flavour during

51

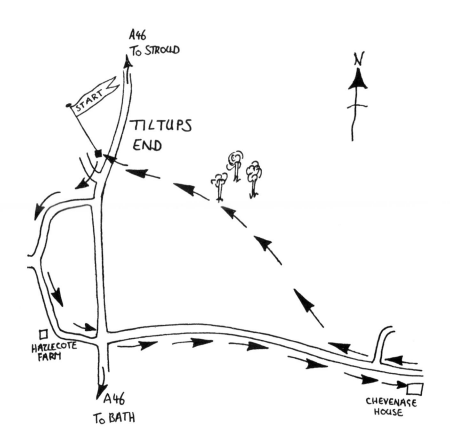

my visit. In the first category you may select from garlic mushrooms, pheasant pâté, soup of the day, jumbo hot dog and chips, ¼ lb burger and chips, gammon and pineapple, mixed grill, steak and ploughman's lunches with a choice of pâté, Stilton, Cheddar and, appropriately double Gloucester. There is also a traditional roast beef Sunday lunch. The inn requests that Sunday walkers call in to order before they set out. The chef's specials include beef and Guinness pie, fisherman's pie, chicken and mushroom pie, lamb and apricot curry, poached local trout and cottage pie. The inn provides facilities for playing darts and pool. There is also a large function room available.

Telephone: Stroud (0453) 832466.

How to get there: Tipputs Inn is on the A46, 4 miles south of Stroud. It is also just over 4 miles from Tetbury, using the A4135 and A46.

Parking: There is a substantial car park at the side and rear of the inn, but it gets busy in summer and on Sundays.

Length of the walk: 6¼ miles. Map: OS Landranger series 162 Gloucester and Forest of Dean (GR 844971).

This is a relatively level walk over the Cotswold plateau but in one part close enough to the escarpment to afford wide views towards the Severn and Vale of Berkeley. The walk passes through Chevenage Green which is close to Chevenage House.

The Walk

From the inn turn right and pass the Q8 garage, taking the second lane to the right past the inn. Walk along this side road, under pylons, with excellent views over to the right. In nearly a mile turn left at the road junction, which has a triangulation station neatly built into the dry-stone wall. You pass through Hazlecote Farm and immediately past it follow the road to the left towards the A46. Cross over, walking down the slope through Cranmore Farm, which at a distance straddles the lane. This is a gated road: the only gate appears to be at Cranmore. You walk ahead down the lane to Chevenage Green. Here the lane is in an avenue of chestnut and lime trees which leads on to Chevenage House on the right. This is an Elizabethan manor house of exceedingly fine proportions, which has Cromwellian associations, although it is said to be haunted by King Charles I. The house is open to the public on Thursdays and Sundays from May to September between 2 pm and 5 pm. It is very well worth a visit and among other items contains some fine 17th century tapestries.

Having visited the house, retrace your steps along the avenue to Chevenage Green where you take the right branch of the route towards Ledgemore Bottom. This bridleway runs gently uphill but descends sharply into the dry valley of Ledgemore Bottom. From here it is just ½ mile further to the A46 and Tiltups End, with the inn across the road from the end of the bridletrack, which is where the walk finishes.

⑬ Slad
The Woolpack Inn

The Woolpack is a tall, stone-built inn, opposite the church in the centre of Slad. In many ways it is a splendidly old-fashioned village pub at which you will get a warm welcome. This is *Cider With Rosie* country, and the inn maintains an exhibition of Laurie Lee's books with signed copies for sale. Additionally, one of the seats on the settle is his and an engraved brass name-plate reserves Laurie Lee his personal seat in the inn next to a signed picture.

The Woolpack is a freehouse which has on draught Wadsworth 6X, Boddingtons Bitter, Flowers Original, Uley Old Spot and Uley Pig's Ear strong beer. This wayside country pub also sells Guinness, Stella Artois and plenty of cider. There is Gresford Press cider, Inches cider (8% alcohol) and Bulmer's traditional draught cider. There is a full range of bottled beer, lagers and soft drinks. The pub also sells wine by the glass, and low-alcohol lagers such as White Label and Kaliber. You can also partake of a 'Cider With Rosie' cocktail which is a strong drink comprising a measure of gin, rosé wine, strong cider and a secret ingredient, served in a long glass with fruit and straws.

There are three small bars and an outside terrace with stupendous views over the valley at the rear of the pub. Beer and food may be taken in all four locations, the range and quality being splendid. As bar snacks you can select from six varieties of jacket potato, ploughman's lunches, toast and pâté, bacon roll, soup and roll, and a range of sandwiches and side salads, but sandwiches and rolls are not available in the evenings or on Sundays.

Main courses vary from time to time but generally include ocean pie, shepherd's pie, macaroni cheese, lasagne, spring lamb and apricot casserole, beef curry, cheesy leek pie, spring vegetable crumble, chilli con carne, chicken curry Madras and chicken tikka masala. Puddings comprise apple pie, death by chocolate, treacle tart, cheesecake and ice-cream. The pub serves food between 12.15 pm and 2.15 pm and 7 pm and 9.30 pm, and closes at 2.30 pm on weekdays, 4 pm on Saturdays and 3 pm on Sundays. Between October and May two real fires burn in the pub's ample hearths. Children and their parents are allowed in the Cider With Rosie bar, which is a family room. Downstairs there is a pool room, with darts and quoits also available. I was delighted to find that there is no music, just very good conversation, and not a chip anywhere on the menu! The inn does not have accommodation, but acts as a clearing house for bed and breakfasts in the village.

Telephone: Gloucester (0452) 813429.

How to get there: Slad is 2½ miles north-east of Stroud along the B4070. It is also within easy reach of both Gloucester and Cheltenham.

Parking: There is a very small car park at the rear of the inn and cars do park on the road in front of the pub. There is also parking available 500 yards up the road in Steanbridge Lane which is off the B4070 to the right.

Length of the walk: 2½ miles. Map: OS Landranger series 162 Gloucester and Forest of Dean (GR 873074).

This is a splendid and bracing walk over and down the valley from Slad in typical Cotswold countryside of the kind found hereabouts. You pass Rosie's cottage and the Slad village school where Laurie Lee was educated. Take a look inside the Victorian Holy Trinity church opposite the pub, with a date on the clock of 1887.

The Walk
From the Woolpack turn right and walk gently uphill along the pavement of this relatively quiet road. You pass the church on the left and just past Well Cottage on the right, bear right into Steanbridge Lane which at first has a gentle downhill slope before it levels out. Follow

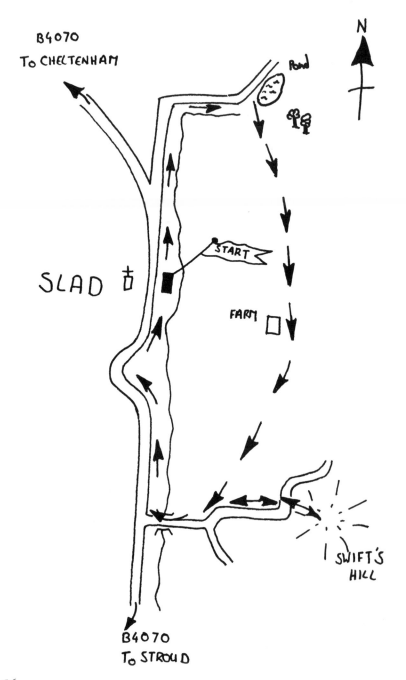

B4070
To CHELTENHAM

Pond

N

SLAD

START

FARM

SWIFT'S
HILL

B4070
To STROUD

the lane sharply round to the right just past Yew Tree Gallery and steeply downhill. You will find yourself walking beside pretty gardens, orchards and paddocks containing hens, geese and beehives. At Cob House Barn bear left along the lane but in 30 yards, with the pond on the right, take the bridleway indicated to the right. A variety of wildlife populates the pond including ducks, moorhen and coots, together with reeds and lilies. Take the stile ahead and follow the small, painted waymarks on this steep uphill stretch with the field boundary kept to the right. There is a good view to be had to the rear just before the stile and the waymark takes you into woodland through which you walk uphill emerging over a stile into a pasture. Walk ahead, keeping the field boundary to the left. Go over another stile walking gently downhill and take a good look at the spectacular view across the valley towards Stroud and to the woodland left and right on the valley tops. You pass through an old orchard where the trees are profuse with clinging mistletoe, and cross two waymarked farm gates; the path now having become a track leading to Furners Farm. Go over the green field gate ahead and down through a newly-planted apple orchard, eschewing the stile on the left but here heading half-right over the field down to a footbrige. This is an area deep in clover and buttercups with May blossom running riot at the correct time of the year. Cross the stream by the bridge and walk half-right up the slope over the pasture. You walk diagonally over this field to a gate, two stiles and waymarks, and walk ahead below the steep embankment which runs along the next field. Swift's Hill is up to the left and at the road junction some way ahead you can make a detour to its summit to view the spectacular panorama it offers, adding in total a mile there and back to the walk.

Head for the row of conifers over to the right and take the stile under the power cables and turn left along the drive to the road ahead. You should turn left here to get to Swift's Hill, otherwise walk another 10 yards and at this junction follow the road round to the right towards The Vatch. In the valley bottom beside a cottage garden and gushing spring take the waymarked path on the right which goes steeply uphill. A stile gives access to the road and you should turn right following the pavement on the right, initially through woodland of ash, beech and sycamore, back to the Woolpack and the car parking area.

14 **Birdlip**
The Air Balloon

Approached along the A417 or the A436, the Air Balloon is in the angle of main roads at the roundabout on the summit of Birdlip Hill. Despite this busy position the walks hereabouts are superb and it is very easy to get away quickly from the traffic. The inn lies back from the road and inside its characterful thick walls is an oasis of quiet.

The history of the inn is that originally it formed two adjacent ale houses which met all the travellers' needs as they toiled up to the crest of the Cotswolds from Gloucester. The first balloon ascents were made about 1784 and from 1796 this inn was called, simply, the Balloon. It did not become the Air Balloon until 1802 and has retained that name since. Around the thick stone walls of the main bar are numerous old prints and paintings of air balloons of all shapes and size. Nowadays, balloon launchings and ascents are made from the grounds of the pub, especially in the summer months.

The range of beer on offer is extensive. Regularly there is draught Flowers Best Bitter and Flowers Original, Wadworth 6X and Boddingtons Bitter. There is also draught Stella Artois, Heineken, Guinness, Strongbow cider and Swan Light. In addition, the inn will offer a selection of ales from Morland Old Speckled Hen, Hook Norton

Brewery's Old Hooky, Archers Gold, Farmer's Glory, or Boddingtons Exhibition. There are also four draught white wines.

Two cosy bars with wood fires, stone walls and low-beamed ceilings are at the core of this pub. Around it are extensive rooms at different levels for dining and drinking and there is additional capacity in a small marquee added to the entrance and in the garden beyond. The Air Balloon has a good menu. Following a range of starters, the main courses include steak and kidney pie, Cumberland sausage, lasagne, roast chicken, a trio of lamb cutlets, and fillet of plaice. For vegetarians there is vegetable lasagne or vegetable samosas and mushroom and nut fettucine. In addition, there are salad platters, four sandwiches and hot steak sandwiches, together with Cheddar ploughman's lunch. Daily specials are listed on a blackboard as are special children's meals and desserts.

In the summer food and drink may be taken outdoors in the gardens where there is also an extensive children's play area. Inside there is a separate children's dining area for the independently minded.

Telephone: Gloucester (0452) 862541.

How to get there: The Air Balloon is easily accessible from Gloucester, Cirencester, Cheltenham or Stroud by way of the A417, A436 or the B4070. Gloucester is 7 miles away and Cheltenham 4 miles. The inn is located at the junction of these three roads where they form a roundabout at the top of Birdlip Hill next to Crickley Hill Country Park.

Parking: There is an ample car park but it fills up quickly at this popular pub and you should ask before you leave your car there while you walk. Another car park lies a few hundred yards south along the A417 in the Country Park on the crest of Birdlip Hill and for any extensive stay this might be the better bet.

Length of the walk: 4 miles. Map: OS Landranger series 163 Cheltenham and Cirencester (GR 935161).

The walk is in scenically exhilarating country on the crest of the Cotswolds near Birdlip Hill and adjacent to Crickley Hill Country Park and close to Great Witcombe Roman Villa. The country park is 144 acres of limestone grassland, beech wood and parkland on the Cotswold escarpment, commanding magnificent views over the Severn Vale to the Forest of Dean and the Welsh hills beyond. On the promontory of the park is the site of an iron age hill fort. Great Witcombe Roman Villa is a short drive from the Air Balloon. It is a large villa, open all the year, and is built round three sides of a courtyard in a beautiful countryside setting.

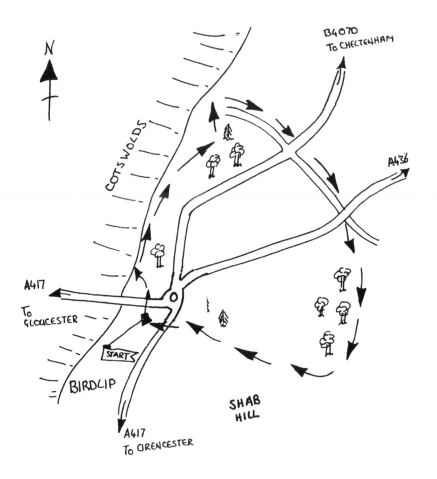

The Walk

From the Air Balloon cross the busy road up from Gloucester to the roundabout. A waymark opposite will take you into the National Trust land on Crickley Hill along part of the Cotswold Way. You walk ahead on a well waymarked path into woodland and uphill. You pass through a gate, rising quite steeply through woods of mature beech and holly. In due course the pathway levels out and you cross a road with a gate on each side. At the far side take the kissing-gate to the right on to Crickley Hill. There are splendid views to be had from here, not just over Gloucester and round to Cheltenham but much further afield to the west. The path goes along the escarpment edge over grassland and in about 400 yards you bear right, keeping along the high ground with the dry-stone wall on the right and plunging into beech woods with waymarks painted on the trunks.

Inside the wood is a series of stiles. Initially you walk gently downhill, then more steeply, bearing right to follow the stone wall on your right. Soon the path rises quite steeply for a short distance and bears left along the edge of a prominent conifer plantation. Stiles take you to the right through the conifers on a gently rising slope but keeping parallel with the edge of the wood. You will see the mound of a long barrow on the right and you might hear the call or cackle of a jay or magpie in the distance. In due course the path bears right, now passing through beech trees alone. You may glimpse a prominent and gnarled beech over in the middle distance: head for it. At this point you emerge over a gate on to a road along which you turn right, now with good views of Cheltenham to the left and soon a view of the Devil's Chimney on the left.

The narrow and quiet lane gently rises to Ullenwood reservoir on the right and the buildings of a camp beyond it. You soon skirt the woods of Ullenwood Court and the lane has begun a gentle descent. At the junction with the B4070 walk ahead towards the National Star Centre, the road still being waymarked as part of the Cotswold Way. You will pass Shipton Connemara Pony Stud and the lodge by the National Star Centre College of Further Education. There is a pretty lake down to the right and the club house of Cotswold Hills Golf Club on the left. Walk along this road until you come to the junction with the A436 Gloucester to Stow-on-the-Wold road. Here you cross over the main road and take the track which bears uphill to the right, signposted towards the Woodland Trust property. This stone track ascends in places moderately steeply for some considerable distance, at first through open land and then with woodland bounded by a dry-stone wall on the right. Still rising, the track passes through woodland on both sides, emerges from it and bends quite sharply to a track junction ahead. With the wood still to the right walk ahead on the level track with the masts on Shab Hill clearly visible.

At a junction of tracks just short of Shab Hill take the walking man waymark to the right (it is the second waymark in a short distance). You walk along a field edge with the boundary and wood to the left. Pass over a stile and a well defined track over an arable field. Two stiles take you across a green lane then over more arable land to the corner of the wood ahead. There you enter the wood by a stile and a waymark and follow the well defined path along the edge then through the wood, emerging by a stile on to the A417. The car park of the Air Balloon is opposite.

⑮ Cleeve Hill
The Rising Sun

The Rising Sun is more than a country pub: it is in fact a country hotel with a restaurant, but has a bar serving all the drinks and refreshments a hungry walker might need. It is also ideally located for walks on and over Cleeve Hill which rises to 1,083 ft above sea level immediately behind the Rising Sun.

The Rising Sun is a Lansbury Hotel which is part of the Whitbread group. In the small bar (about to be enlarged when I was there) you can quench your thirst with Courage Countryside Bitter, Flowers BB, Heineken, Kronenbourg strong lager, Murphy's Irish Stout or Scrumpy Jack strong cider from Symond's. There are low-alcohol lagers such as White Label and Swan Light.

The quite ample snack menu can be taken in the bar while the full à la carte menu pertains only to the restaurant. The snacks you may choose from include soup of the day, which is always home-made, eight types of sandwich, six salad platters and three kinds of ploughman's lunch. There is also a 'fishwich' available and ¼ lb beefburgers. Vegetarian dishes include cauliflower cheese grill, vegetarian lasagne and vegetarian samosas. There is also grilled plaice, tortellini alla carbonara, chicken Kiev and the chef's home-made pie

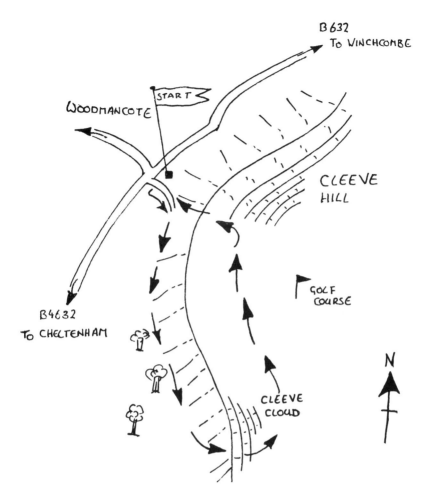

of the day. Puddings are advertised on a separate board. The bar is open from 11 am to 2.30 pm and 6 pm to 11 pm on weekdays, with shorter hours on Sundays. Food is served from noon to 2.30 pm and 6 pm to 9.30 pm (9 pm on Sunday).

Telephone: Cheltenham (0242) 676281.

How to get there: The Rising Sun is on the B4632 (formerly A46) 4 miles north of Cheltenham and 3 miles south-west of Winchcombe. Junction 11 of the M5 is 7 miles away, to the west of Cheltenham.

Parking: The Rising Sun has a large car park but only for patrons of the facilities. It is worthwhile making an arrangement at the hotel desk.

Length of the walk: 3 miles but the walk can be extended to 4½ miles. Map: OS Landranger series 163 Cheltenham and Cirencester (GR 985268).

This walk is on one of the glorious remaining open spaces of Gloucestershire. Cleeve Common now has a golf course on it but the walk along the edge of the Cotswolds on Cleeve Cloud gives one a sense of freedom and timelessness, for you are free to ramble and scramble on the common at will, following a range of waymarked footpaths on this the highest spot on the Cotswold Hills and in the county. There are the remains of ancient earthworks some 350 ft long at Cleeve Cloud and with a good view over to Nottingham Hill where there is another hill fort. So exposed is Cleeve Common that you need to take account of the prevailing weather conditions: the thin layer of clay on top of the limestone can become extremely slippery in the wet, but on a fine, calm day the walking and the immense panorama are exhilarating.

The Walk

From the Rising Sun car park turn left and walk uphill over the cattle grid on to the edge of Cleeve Common. In 100 yards turn right along a waymarked public path, which is a stony track running gently uphill. To the right views soon emerge over Cheltenham and the Severn valley to south and mid-Wales. Above you to the left is the high escarpment of the Cotswolds with limestone outcrops exposed to the west. The track passes unfenced through rough grazing on the common's edge with a substantial beech wood down to the right which may in some circumstances serve both to give shelter from a westerly wind and to muffle the distant noise of the M5 beyond Bishop's Cleeve.

At the end of the wood the track runs round to the right of a small earthwork on a prominent knoll. At this point walk across rough grazing land immediately to the left of the knoll, an unwaymarked path runs obliquely up the escarpment affording spectacular views to the west. Walk uphill ahead and then carefully take a scramble for 20 yards very steeply upwards through the exposed limestone of the escarpment to emerge on the relatively flat top of Cleeve Cloud. Here you will find a broad grass track and you should turn left along it and through the ditches and embankments of the earthwork.

The golf course is over to the right and a waymark by the 14th hole indicates the track ahead along the edge of the escarpment with the dip slope running away to the right. From here there is superb visibility to the west, both up and down the Severn valley to the Brecon Beacons and the Forest of Dean, but beware, for in the wet the innocuous looking turf can be extremely slippery and the view negligible if it is cloudy.

Take the track which runs slightly downhill to the left and away from the golf course and along the escarpment edge. In due course it will run into a gully which may be a further part of the ancient earthwork. You will find a bench seat on the left which is a good spot to take a rest and take in the view. Some 30 yards further the track curves round sharply to the left and runs steeply downhill with the settlement of Cleeve Hill ahead. There are further seats hereabouts maintained, as is the whole area, by the Cleeve Common Board of Conservators. You exit from the common over the cattle grid and return to the Rising Sun car park on the right.

16 Ewen
The Wild Duck Inn

Ewen means spring or source of a river, and it is close to one of the disputed sources of the river Thames which flows as a narrow and shallow brook along the southern edge of the village. The Wild Duck Inn is a family-run freehouse at Drake's Island, Ewen, and dates from 1563. It is a rambling building with considerable charm and stands in a quiet rural setting on the eastern edge of the village. This inn succeeds thoroughly in providing a friendly and comfortable atmosphere, with good food, pleasing ales and fine wines from both Old and New World locations. The inn clearly represents a conversion from what was previously a stone-built house and outbuildings, set in a substantial garden back and front. Consisting of one bar with some four adjacent rooms, there are welcoming wood fires in winter.

The Wild Duck is extremely well furnished in a characterful and inviting manner. Oil portraits line some walls, including pictures of the Prince of Wales and Princess Diana, perhaps tactfully arranged to be at opposite sides of the inn. There is a sheltered garden with a southern aspect for summer use.

The selection of draught beer on offer is impressive and includes domestic beers such as McEwan's Export, Theakston Old Peculier and

XB, Fuller's London Pride and Duckpond Bitter (a beer specially brewed for the Wild Duck by Archers). Guinness and Dry Blackthorn cider are also available. Foreign beers include Coors Extra Gold on draught, Beck's, Carlsberg and Hunter bitter.

Bottled beer continues the international flavour with Coors and Rolling Rock (USA), Molson (Canada), Castle (South Africa), Karel IV (Czechoslovakia), Elephant (Denmark) and Steinlager (New Zealand), to mention but a few of the lines regularly carried. In addition to spirits and soft drinks there is also bottled low-alcohol Kaliber.

The lunchtime and evening menu divides neatly into four parts with a variable series of daily specials, a regular menu, a speciality fish menu and vegetarian fare. Specials often include excellent whole plaice and chips, moules marinière, Cornish scallops and warm salad and Mexican chilli and salad. The regular menu has soup of the day, duck with pear, Thai style beef, escalope of pork with leeks and mushrooms, sirloin, rump and fillet steaks and breast of chicken in brandy with crushed black pepper.

The wide-ranging and speciality fish menu comprises Dover and lemon sole, red mullet, plaice, trout, porbeagle shark, garlic prawns, red bream, parrot fish, barracuda, tuna loin, sturgeon fillet, red snapper, John Dory, American bass and salmon steaks, while vegetarians may select from mushroom Stroganov with savoury rice, vegetarian sausages with Yorkshire pudding and onions, ploughman's lunches with Brie, Stilton or Cheddar, and mushroom quiche with salad. The standard of the food and the beer is outstandingly good.

Food hours are noon to 2 pm and 6.45 pm to 10 pm on weekdays and noon to 2 pm and 7 pm to 9.45 pm on Sundays. The bar only is open on Christmas Day, and be warned, unattended children will be sold as slaves! The Wild Duck has residential accommodation with en suite rooms all with colour TV and tea/coffee making facilities. Two of these rooms in the oldest part of the building are furnished in four-poster style.

Telephone: Cirencester (0285) 770310 or 770364.

How to get there: The Wild Duck lies some 4 miles south-west of Cirencester, a mile off the A429 Cirencester to Malmesbury road and a mile east of Kemble.

Parking: There is a large car park at the front of the inn.

Length of the walk: 4 miles. Map: OS Landranger series 163 Cheltenham and Cirencester (GR 006975).

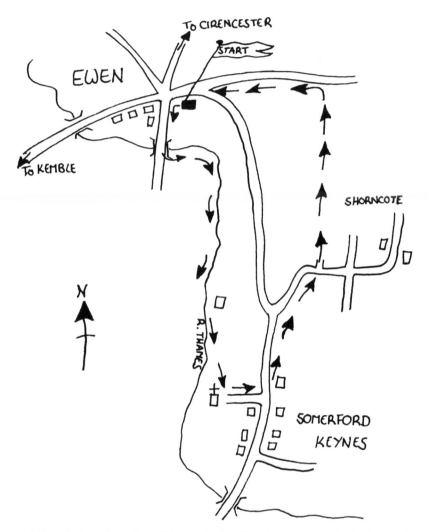

Although Ewen is a Cotswold stone-built village it verges on the border of the north Wiltshire clay vale: consequently this is easy going and level walking country but it may be wet along the stripling Thames.

Gardens in Ewen open for one day, usually in July (details in the National Gardens Scheme book). Brooke House used to be the kitchen garden of Ewen Manor and has a walled garden with roses, shrubberies and herbaceous borders. Ewen Manor house is not open to the public but the garden has a lily pool, cedars, yews and a sunken garden. The Cotswold Water Park is nearby and covers many acres and affords some 80 lakes for bird-watching and water sports.

The Walk

Turn left from the Wild Duck and walk through Ewen along the picturesque village street. At the road junction turn left towards Poole Keynes and Oaksey, passing further Cotswold stone cottages and farms. At the stripling Thames cross the bridge but immediately take the waymarked footpath and stile beside the watercourse on the left. You cross the pasture obliquely to a field gate then walk over the next field in the same broadly diagonal direction to a gateway under the double power lines. You walk ahead to a stile in the corner of the field. The Thames will now be on your left. Follow this relatively fast flowing stream in all its varied moods to Upper Mill Farm.

Cross a weir over the mill race and pass through a corner of Upper Mill garden from which you exit by way of a stile and follow the waymarked path to Somerford Keynes. Walk across the field ahead, passing just left of the windpump to a gate in the hedgerow beyond. You will find a stile and a waymark which will direct you ahead, keeping the hedgerow to your left. Take the waymarked path over a stile, turning left in some 600 yards: in a further 40 yards turn right, cross a stile, bear half-left and walk to the corner of the field along a well-worn footpath where you will find another stile to cross. Somerford Keynes is now well in view. Follow the wall on your right and quickly cross a further stile. The village church is over to the right. Follow the path into the village, joining the road through a gate and walk to the left. In a few yards turn left at the road junction. It is perhaps worth while knowing that the Baker's Arms in Somerford Keynes, a freehouse serving food and ales, is some 500 yards in the opposite direction at this point.

On your right pass Elm View and in 150 yards a road branches off to the left to Ewen and Kemble. Walk ahead ignoring both junctions, travelling in the Siddington direction. In due course the road turns sharply right. At this point take the unwaymarked track on the left. It is a broad, largely dry, unadopted enclosure road. In slightly under a mile a wood will appear on the left and in a couple of hundred yards the track ends at the South Cerney to Ewen road. Turn left and walk back to the Wild Duck.

Winchcombe
The Corner Cupboard Inn

The distinctive name of this delightful family-run Flowers inn derives from the corner cupboards which still remain around its walls. There were several but when successive landlords ran up against hard times they were sold off one by one to pay the debts: two remain. This characterful inn was built some time in the late 13th century and became a farmhouse for a time, then under the charge of John Durham who started the paper mills in Winchcombe. It was a pub certainly from 1876 and the fact that its side faces Malthouse Lane tells more about the inn's provenance.

There are two bars: the old smoke room and the lounge complete with original oak beams and an inglenook fireplace. The lounge was constructed from stone which came from Winchcombe Abbey after its dissolution by Henry VIII, and the walls are lined with photographs, paintings and prints of Winchcombe. There are tables and chairs in the bars as well as a separate dining area; there is a small functions room. Walking parties of 10 or so can book the dining area if they telephone ahead of their visit.

The inn is distinctive and so is the menu, which consists entirely of attractive home-made food. This forms an excellent complement to the real ales on offer. There is Boddingtons Bitter, Castle Eden Ale, Hook Norton BB, Flowers Original, Marston's Pedigree and Whitbread BB on tap. In addition you may order draught Guinness, Murphy's Irish Stout, Stella Artois, Heineken, Weston's Old Rosie Cider, Bulmer's Traditional Cider and Dry Blackthorn. There is an ample range of low-alcohol lagers and also coffee.

The menu is advertised on blackboards and changes quite often. You may have curried parsnip soup or cream of watercress, followed by such dishes as game pie and fresh vegetables, honey roast ham and parsley sauce, hot and fruity chicken curry and rice, sausages, mash and mushy peas, baked avocado with Stilton and walnuts, sirloin steak, rollmops with apple, celery and onion salad. There are certain dishes which will be provided on request such as a variety of omelettes. Vegetarian dishes include spinach and mushroom crêpes and leek and potato pie. There is not a single chip on the menu!

Snacks include venison liver pâté with brandy, served with toast. There are also ploughman's lunches, drover's lunch, fisherman's lunch and countryman's lunch. Puddings, on a separate list, include apple flapjack pudding, pear frangipane tart and walnut fudge tart. There is a secluded garden which caters for a mixture of locals and visitors. You may play dominoes, scrabble, cards or monopoly but not a juke-box!

The pub ghost is said to be a young girl aged about twelve: she has been heard, her footsteps patter from time to time, and once she is said to have upset a collection of Victorian dolls in the pub which were up for sale.

Telephone: Cheltenham (0242) 602303.

How to get there: Winchcombe is on the B4632, 7 miles north-east of Cheltenham and 9 miles from Evesham on the B4078. The village can be reached from the A40 east of Cheltenham by turning off at Andoversford and using minor roads through Brockhampton. The inn is in Gloucester Street, the main route running through Winchcombe, and at the southern end of the settlement.

Parking: There is a small car park at the inn and spaces in Gloucester Street, and Back Lane, where there is also a long-stay car park.

Length of the walk: 4½ miles. The extension to Belas Knap Long Barrow will add another 2 miles. Map: OS Landranger series 163 Cheltenham and Cirencester (GR 019279).

This splendid village was once the walled capital of Winchcombeshire and grew up around the Abbey. It is an excellent starting point for this walk which has been

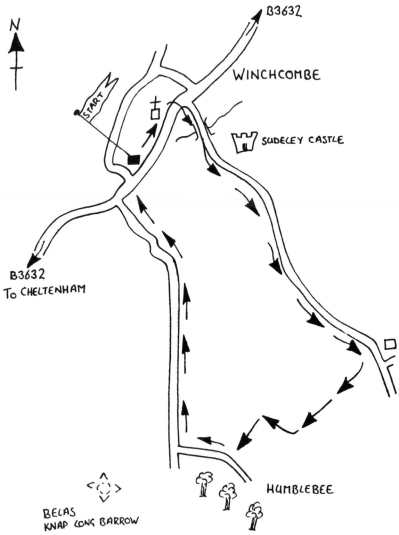

N

B3632

WINCHCOMBE

START

SUDELEY CASTLE

B3632
To CHELTENHAM

<^>
<(.)>
<v>

BELAS
KNAP LONG BARROW

HUMBLEBEE

selected from the myriad of footpaths in the area and represents a relatively
straightforward all-weather walk. The walk passes Sudeley Castle (which is open daily
from April to the end of October) and the Long Barrow of Belas Knap is a mile away.

The Walk

Turn left from the Corner Cupboard Inn and walk down Gloucester
Street towards the church. Pass through Queen's Square turning right
into the Vineyard, crossing the upper water of the river Isbourne. You

are now into open country in a lime avenue which leads to the entrance of Sudeley Castle but bear right along the metalled lane which ends 1½ miles away in tracks. You walk between low quickthorn hedges. There is a waymarked footpath to the right in due course towards Humblebee. It forms part of the Cotswold Way but passes over ploughed fields which may be difficult in certain conditions. You may take it if you wish, but the preferred route is ahead on this undulating lane with Sudeley Castle on its knoll over to the left.

The lane turns through oak and ash woods and runs unfenced gently uphill offering good all-round views. Passing secluded Lanes Cottage, the lane then runs downhill with a pond and farm to the left: you may hear coot, moorhen and duck before they come into sight. At New Meadow and New Meadow Barn turn right over the gate up the track so obviously posted as unsuitable for motor vehicles. Walk ahead uphill along the track, in due course crossing a gate and continuing uphill. The track levels out with a wood ahead and to the right. At the wood turn right through a gate along another track. Superb views are to be had over the neighbouring valley, particularly in the morning sun.

The track now rises with the wood to the left and you will come to a pair of cottages on the left, well built from dressed stone. Immediately past the cottages turn left up the waymarked track which runs uphill quite steeply. At the road turn right along the waymark which indicates that this is again part of the Cotswold Way. Humblebee Wood is now to the left and behind you.

This quiet lane now runs downhill quite steeply through woodland and hereabouts Winchcombe comes into sight ahead and to the right. The Cotswold Way leaves the lane to the left and it is here that you may join it to make the detour to Belas Knap Long Barrow if you so wish, otherwise walk ahead down the lane turning right at the junction. The signpost indicates Winchcombe to be 2 miles away but maybe the steep downhill slope gives one the impression that it is closer than that distance.

The lane levels out past Wadfield House and Farm and Sudeley Castle again comes into sight half-right and about ¾ mile away. The walk goes gently downhill passing the entrance to Corndean Hall on the left. You pass a wood on the right then enter the settlement of Winchcombe. At Lark Rise you may take the footpath over the stone stile to the right which passes over a meadow to the church, alternatively follow the road to the left walking back over the river and out of Corndean Lane. Turn right into Winchcombe passing the hospital on the left and along the Cheltenham road to the Corner Cupboard Inn on the left.

⓲ Brockhampton
The Craven Arms

This interesting 17th century freehouse is near the end of one of Brockhampton's village streets. Approached from the rear by way of the car park, there is a small garden to which you may take your drink. Inside, there are two bars and several rooms for both eating and drinking.

There is a good selection of draught beer on offer ranging from Wadworth 6X to Murphy's Irish Stout and including Hook Norton Bitter, Butcombe Bitter from Bristol, John Smith's Yorkshire Bitter, Worthington Best Bitter, and in the lager category there is Stella Artois and Carlsberg. The Craven Arms also offers Beck's Bitter and a wide range of soft and non-alcoholic drinks.

The menu is varied and comprises a number of lunchtime bar meals and a series of evening snacks and substantial meals. You may have soup of the day, jumbo sausage roll and chips, fillet of plaice or haddock and chips, beef curry, a large ploughman's salad, curried chicken, lasagne and home-made steak and kidney pie. To follow there is a range of home-made sweets and various ice-creams. The full evening menu includes prime Scottish sirloin steak, king prawns with garlic butter and brown bread, avocado salad with Alabama sauce and breaded scampi. There is fillet of sole, Dundee lamb, poached salmon, roast duck, chicken and Stilton, Scottish fillet and prime Scottish sirloin and beef bourguignonne. The wine list is extensive.

Beyond the car park there is a sizeable children's play area facing into the fields and away from the village but very much in view of the beer garden.

Telephone: Cheltenham (0242) 820410.

How to get there: Turn north from the A40 at Andoversford along the A436. Take the turning to Syreford and Brockhampton on the country road which leads up to Winchcombe.

Parking: There are spaces in the pub car park, and it may also be possible to park near the pub in the village street.

Length of the walk: 2 miles. Map: OS Landranger series 163 Cheltenham and Cirencester (GR 035223).

The scenery offered by this walk is quite typical of this part of the Cotswolds; at one moment giving extensive views over the rolling upland, at the next enfolded in deep and narrow valleys. This relatively short walk takes in the village of Brockhampton and extends down the valley as far as Sevenhampton. If you have the chance, take a look at the impressive Brockhampton Park which is away from the walk on the Winchcombe to Andoversford road. Sevenhampton church and the neighbouring Jacobean manor house are both on the route of the walk.

The Walk

From the pub car park turn right along the village road, the way you drove up to the Craven Arms. At the junction near the Old Shop bed and breakfast turn right again. Just past the chapel take another right along a narrow lane which runs as an easy walk above the valley and gives all-round views. There is a series of seats along the verge for those who wish to rest and to take in the local landscape views. You will pass Sevenhampton church, which is across the valley, but the village itself spans the stream and climbs up both sides of the valley dotted with a series of stone houses and cottages running up to the swelling hills. It is an attractive village.

At the telephone box turn right down to the stream but at the ford take the waymarked footpath to Brockhampton via St Andrew's church. There is a narrow footbridge over the stream with a stile which leads uphill to a small gate. You cross the paddock to the church. Cross over the road and the footpath goes through the churchyard. The central tower has interesting internal flying buttresses, the building being of a simple nave and chancel pattern

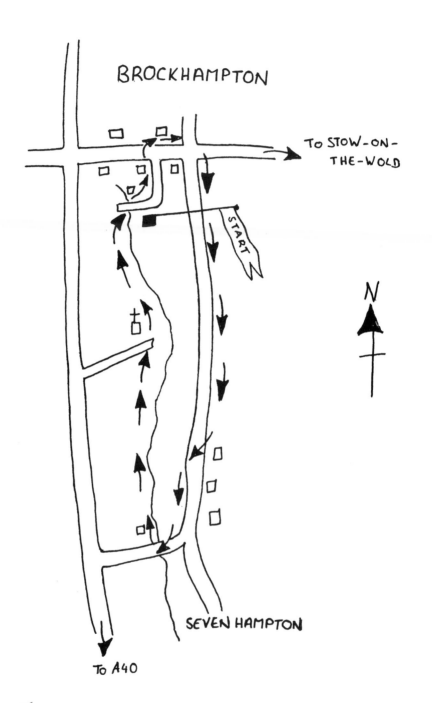

BROCKHAMPTON

TO STOW-ON-
THE-WOLD

START

N

SEVEN HAMPTON

TO A40

with an aisle on each side. There is a fine brass portrait of John Camber in the church. He was a wealthy wool merchant and benefactor of the church who died in 1497 and is shown with a purse at his waist, fur-trimmed sleeves, long hair and praying hands.

The footpath exits in the north-east of the churchyard by a kissing-gate. With the wall to your left, walk at first gently downhill, then uphill. Keep your eyes open here for the occasional heron which may be disturbed from the stream by your approach. Go through the gate on the waymarked path and ahead across the field but head a little to the right of the centre. You will find a waymark in 100 yards on a pole carrying electricity wires. Edge gradually down towards the stream, cross the gate and bridge. There is a series of springs to right and left marking the source of this stream and above the valley floor is the obvious outline on the right of the old brewery, clearly located to take advantage of plentiful, pure, free water from the springs hereabouts. The Craven Arms is on the right only some 10 yards further along the street.

⑲ Withington
The Mill Inn

This pub is beautifully situated on the upper waters of the river Colne which flows through the grounds. It is a low-beamed and dark, characterful inn with a range of adjoining buildings clearly associated with its former use from which the pub now takes its name. This Samuel Smith house serves a range of the brewery's bitter: Old Brewery Bitter, Museum Ale, Sovereign Best Bitter and 4X Best Bitter along with Samuel Smith Cider Reserve. There is also dark milk and extra stout available along with Ayingerbrau lager, Prinz lager, Diet Pils strong lager and a low-alcohol lager, with a full range of soft drinks and coffee. The Mill Inn has a good menu including soup, jacket potato, ploughman's lunches, basket meals, children's food and vegetarian meals. The menu centres on house specials such as home-made steak and kidney pie, seafood platter, home-made lasagne, grilled trout and almonds and sirloin steak. Sunday lunch, served only between noon and 2.30 pm, comprises roast beef or lamb served with new or roast potatoes, vegetables, Yorkshire pudding and gravy. The inn caters for special events, and rooms are available on a bed and breakfast basis all the year round. There is a large garden at the side of the inn and across the river Coln on the island.

Telephone: Cheltenham (0242) 890204.

How to get there: Withington is between the A40 Cheltenham to Burford road and the A435 Cheltenham to Cirencester road, some 10 miles from Cirencester and 10 miles from Cheltenham. Turn off the A435 at Colesbourne and the A40 near Compton Abdale or Andoversford. The Mill Inn is at the southern end of the village of Withington.

Parking: The inn car park is extensive but needs extreme care on entering and leaving as it is at a narrow corner.

Length of the walk: 4 miles. Map: OS Landranger series 163 Cheltenham and Cirencester (GR 033153).

Withington is a very pleasant starting point for this walk of some considerable variety extending into the surrounding hills and through Withington Woods. There is an abundance of wildlife and it is perhaps a good walk for spring, a fine summer's morning or in autumn when the cooling canopy of branches offers some respite from the heat of the day. In winter and wet weather be well prepared for mud on the woodland footpaths.

The Walk
From the Mill Inn turn right and follow the road taking the bridge over the river Coln. In 300 yards up the slope turn left along the metalled lane to Halewood on the Chedworth road. At the junction turn left and follow the road. In about 100 yards take a footpath to the right across the fields running uphill towards the electricity pylons. Walk across the immediate brow to a hedge and stile. Here the footpath divides and you take the right branch which ascends the hill slope to the right of Withington Woods. It is in places a steep climb but with

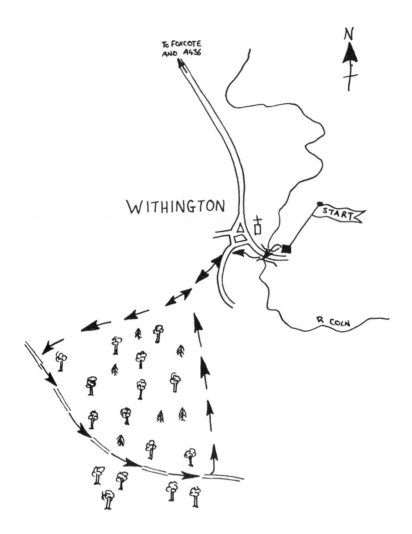

waymarking along the side of woodland over a series of gates and fences.

At the top of the slope a hunt fence is adjacent to a stile and the route is waymarked ahead. Here the woodland retreats to the left. Walk ahead over a field, keeping the boundary hedge on your right. There are extensive breeding and rearing pens for the profusion of pheasants which populate this area and the adjacent woodland in the next field to your right. In due course a well used bridleroad crosses the footpath along which you turn left.

Walking uphill into Withington Woods you pass through conifers, beech, hazel and a withybed. Cross a gate at the edge of this particular part of the wood and walk along the field edge ahead, keeping the hedge to the right. At the far end of the field cross another gate and re-enter the wood along a well-defined bridleway. There is a poplar plantation on the right and the track winds gently to the left through the woodland, running down into a slight hollow. At that point leave the bridleway to the left along a waymarked path which gently undulates through close woodland then mature conifers.

At a junction of paths take the waymarked track which runs generally in the same direction as you have come. The track runs downhill through a selection of mature woodland and coppice. At the edge of the wood cross the gate into the field but keep to the left along the wood's boundary for 20 yards where the path is waymarked over a stile, again following the wood on the left until you come to a hedge and wall. Here bear half-right and walk down under the pylons to rejoin the path which you used to walk out of Withington village. Hereabouts keep a lively ear and eye on the alert, for a plaintive 'pwew' gave me an excellent view of a pair of buzzards wheeling above the valley.

Return to the Mill Inn, using the outward route in reverse, or alternatively it is worthwhile making a slight detour to visit the church of St Michael and All Angels. It is an interesting nave and chancel building with a central tower and a small south chapel. In the Easter sepulchre in the chancel is a stone commemorating one John Stockwell who died of plague, 24th September 1665. Elsewhere is a memorial to W.S. Morrison, Viscount Dunrossil, who was Speaker of the House of Commons and the local Member of Parliament who lived in the manor house here until he became Governor General of Australia. He died in office and is buried in Canberra. Return from the church steeply downhill to the river Coln and the Mill Inn car park.

⟨20⟩ Ford
The Plough Inn

The Plough Inn is one of those rambling stone buildings, more reminiscent of a small farm than a pub, indeed it may have been just that in time gone by. Located at the eastern end of the village of Ford, which sits astride the B4077 where it crosses one of the tributary waters of the river Windrush, the Plough Inn is constructed from Cotswold stone, which also offers an excellent roofing material for this largely 17th century building.

There are two cosy bars with stone floors and three larger rooms off for both drinking and eating, with welcoming wood fires and tastefully quiet background music. Shove-halfpenny is played by the regulars in a local league; horseracing prints and memorabilia adorn the walls.

This is a Donnington Brewery inn and sells its Draught Bitter, Best Bitter and SBA, but also Addlestone's Draught cider (made by Gaymers), Carlsberg lager, Carlsberg Export and Guinness.

The attractive and extensive menu, written on blackboards, is at the pub entrance. There is a selection of home-made soups – onion, beef, leek and potato. On offer is smoked mackerel pâté with toast and salad, chilli con carne, Madras curried beef and home-made lasagne with salad and garlic roll. The main courses include fresh salmon steak, knuckle of lamb cooked with garlic, vegetable and lentil hotpot, home-made steak and kidney pie, liver and bacon casserole and beef bourguignonne. The steaks are itemised as fantastic fillet, super sirloin and prime rump. There is also fillet of beef Napoleon (fillet steak in pudding pastry).

The Plough has a good wine list intending to offer its customers quality wines at drinkable prices, with some wines of the week on special offer. There is live jazz in the evening every second Tuesday in the month.

Accommodation comprises three rooms which can be used as single or double. Dogs, children and mother-in-law are most welcome and the inn serves afternoon teas from Easter to October and English breakfasts every day. There is a car park behind the inn and parking space across the road from the inn. The Plough has a beer garden at the rear.

Telephone: Stanton (0386) 73215.

How to get there: Ford lies 7 miles north-west of Stow-on-the-Wold and 7 miles south of Broadway on the B4077.

Parking: There is a car park at the rear of the inn and space across the B4077 opposite the inn.

Length of the walk: 4¼ miles. Map: OS Landranger series 163 Cheltenham and Cirencester (GR 088294).

This is a relatively gentle walk with two areas of steep uphill walking. It takes in two tributaries which form the upper waters of the river Windrush, set here in deep limestone valleys. An added attraction is the village of Temple Guiting through which the walk passes.

The Walk
Turn right from the Plough along the B4077. There is a deep valley to the right. In some 400 yards take the waymarked footpath leading off the road to the right. It winds round the eastern edge of the valley. You pass over a stile in 100 yards and follow the field edge. This path soon develops into a bridleway giving level walking and good views over and up the valley.

Entering Temple Guiting the track becomes a road. At the junction turn right and downhill. Guiting Park is to the left and the road crosses the lake with a sluice taking the water underneath. You then wind up the opposite side of the valley.

St Mary's church to the left is well worth inspection. It is a honey-

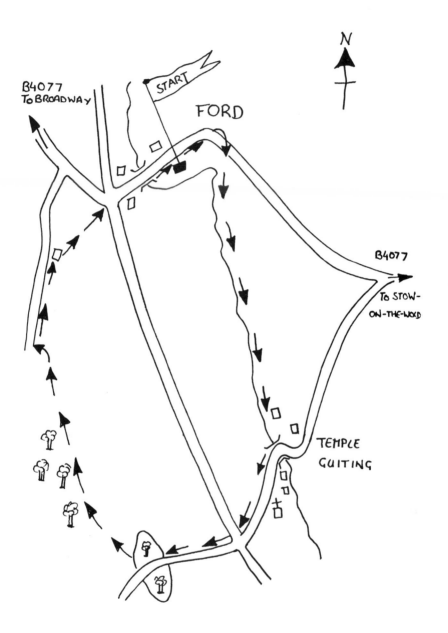

START

B4077
To BROADWAY

FORD

N

B4077
To STOW-
ON-THE-WOLD

TEMPLE
GUITING

coloured stone nave and chancel building with a western tower and small north transept. There are masons' marks on the wall with dates 1645, 1662 and 1762 and an excellent royal coat of arms at the western end of the nave.

Leaving the church take the narrow footpath to the left opposite Shepherd's Cottage which leads to the Ford to Kineton minor road. Take a quick left and right so that you are walking increasingly uphill along the road labelled as unsuitable for motors. It passes through extensive beech, holly and yew. The woodland hilltop provides an excellent resting point with extensive views now appearing over the valley to the west.

In 15 yards take the waymarked bridlepath to the right. The route passes through a series of waymarked gates and stiles over inviting and short-clipped pastures, at first gently rising, then bearing right and losing height down the valley side. Keep your eyes and ears open for the sound of the jay which might evidence itself in the neighbouring woodland.

Pinnock Farm buildings are ahead as you now walk steadily down into the valley with a trilling stream to the left. Cross the stream at a junction of paths but follow the track round to the left and uphill to a gate. Cross the metalled farm road and take the footpath ahead. At the Ford to Winchcombe road turn right along it until you reach Slade Barn Farm where you take the waymarked footpath through a gate to the right. Follow the path uphill keeping the deep stone quarry on the left. In due course keep to the right of the hedgerow, now walking quite steeply uphill to the brow of the hill with the stone quarry immediately to the left. There are extensive views ahead into the middle distance beyond Ford and the racehorse gallops. Follow the field boundary downhill to the west end of Ford, then walk back to the Plough Inn through the village.

21 Hazleton
Puesdown Inn

The ancient and haunted Puesdown Inn, high on the Cotswolds, lies on the northern side of the A40 in somewhat bleak and open countryside. There has been an inn here to greet the weary traveller since 1246, but the inn probably had its heyday in the era of the stagecoach, and was a convenient coaching house on the turnpike road from Cheltenham to Oxford, leading on to London. The road is even busier today and the Puesdown Inn makes a welcome break for the motorist. On my visit to the inn I was not privileged to meet the Puesdown ghost of a highwayman said to have been shot in the doorway of the pub and alleged to reappear from time to time: perhaps you will see him on your visit!

Inside, a model of the inn as an old-time coaching house is preserved in a glass case mounted on a wall: there are other countryside artefacts – saddlery, hay knives and saws, together with horse-racing and hunting photographs and prints.

Tastefully decorated, Puesdown Inn is a spacious place consisting of two connected bars, two large eating areas and a games room in which are a pool table, darts board and fruit machines. Music is at low volume and there are open wood fires in winter.

This freehouse has a good range of beers on draught from the relatively local Hook Norton Best Bitter and Donnington Best Bitter to the more distant beers from Everards Brewery founded in Leicestershire in 1849. It serves Beacon Bitter, Tiger BB and Old Original from Everards. Also on draught are Carlsberg lager and Carlsberg Export, Guinness, Strongbow and Woodpecker cider. There is an extensive wine list.

All tastes seem to be catered for in the varied menu which includes ploughman's with Stilton, Cheddar or home-cooked ham and baguettes with prawn, beef, ham or steak. There is leek and potato soup, whitebait and avocado mousse. Hot meals include home-made lasagne, grilled sirloin steak and garlic, baked salmon, roast haunch of venison, lamb cutlets, chicken korma and casserole of game.   Sweets are especially tempting and include such delights as fresh lemon mousse, bread and butter pudding, banana boat, brandy crème brûlée, with ice-cream, sorbets and coffee. The Puesdown Inn serves meals between 12 noon and 2.30 pm, 6.30 pm and 9 pm. The bar closes during the afternoon except on Saturdays, when it is open from 11 am to 11 pm. Accommodation comprises two double rooms.

Telephone: Cotswold (0451) 860262.

How to get there: The Puesdown Inn is 3 miles west of Northleach and 10 miles east of Cheltenham on the northern side of the A40.

Parking: There is extensive parking space available in front and at the side of the inn.

Length of the walk: 5¾ miles. Map: OS Landranger series 163 Cheltenham and Cirencester (GR 075171).

This undulating walk passes over typical Cotswold countryside and through the villages of Hazleton and Turkdean. Puesdown Inn lies exposed to the elements some 800 ft high on the Cotswolds: Hazleton, whose name means 'tun among the hazels' or 'hazel valley', is much more sheltered while Upper and Lower Turkdean have the full benefit of being enfolded by the hills. Turkdean means 'in the valley of the river Turc', and Turc literally means 'boar'. The name is said to refer to rivers which form deep channels or holes in which they sink into the earth and are lost for a distance, a characteristic typical of limestone countryside.

The Walk

Turn left outside the Puesdown Inn from the car park and walk for 40 yards along the side of the A40 on a broad grass verge. A bridleway branches to the left from the main road. In due course take the waymarked footpath to the left towards Hazleton, keeping the

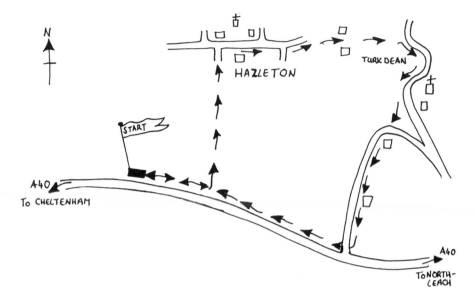

dry-stone wall on the right. The path undulates gently, running down to a triangular-shaped wood on the left then rising gently towards the farm buildings of Hazleton. At the road, turn right: St Andrew's church lies to one side, but you walk ahead through the village on a gentle downhill slope. Passing a sign announcing that this road is now unsuitable for motors, it very soon degenerates into a track. Towards the foot of the slope you pass through a farmyard and onwards down the same dry valley. In some 200 yards a spring emerges on the left and gives rise to a stream which flows along one side of the walk. You will soon reach a copse on the left at which point the stream crosses to the other side of the track.

As you continue an area of woodland appears on the right stretching up the slope. You follow the path to the right through the gate and into the woods, which is quite clearly waymarked uphill through the conifers. You emerge from the wood over a stile at a game fence and turn just half-left to walk across the field ahead but rounding the left corner of the woodland which appears over the immediate horizon. Follow the waymark on the left side of the wood then walk downhill to a small gate across the field ahead. At the gate you re-cross the stream and turn half-right up the slope to join the track which you follow to your right. At a further field gate take the track ahead which goes gently up the slope to farm buildings: Turkdean comes into view on the right. At the road turn right along it and walk through the village. It winds to the right, you pass The Old Shop bed and breakfast on the left, then the road plunges downhill. Turkdean church is to the left. This nave and chancel church with a south aisle and western tower is a mixture of Norman and early English work, but with a Victorianised chancel and brightly painted screen. There are fragments of wall paintings high on the nave.

At the edge of the village, as the road turns left, take a footpath to the right which is not waymarked. It curves very steeply downhill in a narrow ravine. At the hill foot, by a house and buildings across an extensive garden, the path crosses a stream beside a ford to join another road ahead, along which you walk uphill. In due course a virtually all-round panorama comes into view in the neighbourhood of Castle Barn Farm, by which time the slope of the road has levelled out.

Bordering the road, woodland extends along the right, at the end of which you turn right towards Hazleton. This road is sheltered on the left by further woodland from the western end of the Northleach bypass. Where the road turns right, take the track ahead and follow it for 1½ miles to Puesdown Inn.

Barnsley
The Village Pub

22

Barnsley is a splendid stone-built village, described with some accuracy in the *Architectural Review* as one of the most memorable places in England. The Norman church rises above the village.

The Village Pub is a delightful stone-built freehouse standing on the main street, which formed part of the Welsh Way, a long-distance drovers' road running from the Welsh border to Fairford and Lechlade, then on to London. Flocks and herds of animals on the hoof have given way to motor traffic on this portion of the Cirencester to Burford road, but the Village Pub provides an excellent stopping-off point with several walks possible in the vicinity.

Inside, the Village Pub consists of one bar and two cosy dining-rooms at each side, all under low, beamed ceilings. Draught beers served include Beamish Irish Stout, Guinness, Flowers BB and IPA, Wadworth 6X, Heineken and Stella Artois. Kaliber and White Label low-alcohol bottled lagers are available. There is also sweet and dry Bland's West Country cider and a series of speciality fruit wines and country wines, together with an extensive conventional wine list.

The lunch menu is attractive and varied. Farmhouse soup, grilled goat's cheese and grilled fresh sardines are among the starters. Main courses are lasagne, cauliflower cheese, cream cheese and spinach, shepherd's pie and pasta with mushrooms. In addition there are substantial bar snacks, such as ploughman's with ·Stilton, Cheddar, Brie, Camembert, or pâté. Also available is straightforward bread and cheese, open sandwiches, salads and coffee.

Sweets are delicious and appetizing. Home-made apple pie with cream or custard, fresh fruit pavlova, sherry trifle, elderflower syllabub, blackcurrant mousse and raspberry charlotte are among the possibilities.

In the evenings a separate menu operates comprising such items as deep fried Brie, beef in Guinness, chicken chasseur, 10 oz rump steaks, leek and mushroom pie, peppered pork steaks and grilled whole plaice.

There is a garden with tables behind the inn, adjacent to the car park, where summer al fresco food and drink may be consumed: children are allowed into the dining-rooms but not the bar. The Village Pub opens between 11 am and 2.30 pm and 6 pm and 11 pm on weekdays. Sunday hours are 12 noon to 3 pm and 7 pm to 10.30 pm. In the evenings the dining-rooms operate from 7 pm to 9 pm on weekdays and 7 pm to 9.30 pm on Saturdays. The Village Pub offers five rooms for accommodation, four being en suite. This is a pleasant inn which will provide welcome sustenance at the end of an interesting countryside walk.

Telephone: Cirencester (0285) 740421.

How to get there: The Village Pub is on the B4425, 4 miles from Cirencester and 2½ miles from Bibury.

Parking: There is a good car park behind the inn for patrons, whilst parking is quite possible in the village but away from the B4425.

Length of the walk: 3 miles and 5½ miles. Map: OS Landranger series 163 Cheltenham and Cirencester (GR 076051).

This is a flat and easy walk passing through Barnsley Park and around the neighbouring countryside. Barnsley Park has at its centre the 17th century house in a Georgian Baroque style and surrounded by attractive wooded parkland. Its library once contained numerous volumes from Sir Isaac Newton's collection but these now reside elsewhere. Barnsley House garden is open to the public in summer. The re-designed garden contains 18th century summer-houses and is known for its laburnum walk, pond garden, kitchen and herb gardens.

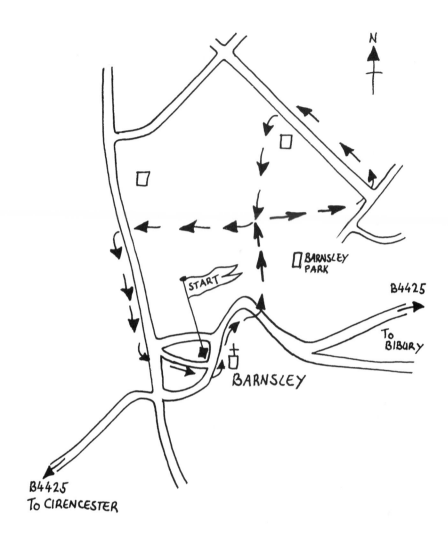

The Walk

Two walks in a figure of eight are possible. For both turn left from the Village Pub along the B4425, passing near the stone-built school, manor and church. At the village edge turn left from the road along a waymarked footpath over a stone stile. This path crosses the ornamentally wooded Barnsley Park over gently rolling countryside. Coming to a driveway, which you follow for a few yards, the path then bears slightly left over a gate then round the ha-ha of Barnsley Park. The house is close to the right and is framed neatly for the

92

photographer by a deeply wooded avenue. The path crosses a further gate beyond the ha-ha and turns immediately right along a track which leads to Barnsley Park stable block. In a short distance, just beyond the lodge on the left, take the metal pedestrian gate to the left and cross a small orchard and two further gates beyond. The path is unmarked over Barnsley Park so some skilled map reading is necessary, but broadly bear gently right after the second gate, walking to keep the stone wall which runs parallel with the path some 50 yards to the right. The path soon crosses a stone stile and heads in the same direction over the park to the high boundary wall a good distance ahead. Keep your eye open for a broad gate in this wall as the stile is just to the left of it. The wall is high and the stile is mounted over a large vertical stone at the top but with easy footholds set into each side of the wall: the stile looks daunting but in reality it is not, unless you are wearing unsuitably tight clothing or have a rheumatic tendency.

Over the stile is a bridlepath running left and right. *For the shorter walk*, turn left and follow the directions as described in the final paragraph. *For the longer walk*, turn right and gently down the slope. The track enters Cadmore Copse in which you bear left through the woodland. This area is near the headwater of a stream which flows down to the river Coln and can be wet and muddy at certain times of the year. In due course the track emerges from the copse with open farmland on the left but woodland still hugging the right. Leaving the wood, cross a gate and walk ahead along a distinct stone track to the road where you continue ahead for a few steps, keeping the farmhouse on the right. Follow the road as it turns left and continue for some ¾ mile along it, passing between hedges and ash trees. On the map is Potato Barn to the left, but on the ground it is renamed Cripp's Barn. A few yards along the road past the lane to the barn is a waymarked footpath to the left. This passes along the field edge towards woodland: Cripp's Barn is now some 250 yards left.

At an unwaymarked junction of tracks, walk ahead but slightly right over pasture, keeping the boundary dry-stone wall and hedge to the right. You come to a gate in the wall which takes the waymarked footpath into the right-hand field. Head for the wall ahead: it has a stile in the centre of the field. The path then crosses the field ahead and exits to the bridlepath some 50 yards from the right-hand corner of the field. At this point the walk is at the high stile over Barnsley Park wall where the short and longer walk diverged. One now has the choice of returning the way one came directly over Barnsley Park or turning right along the bridleway. In the latter case the *directions for both short and longer walk now coincide*.

There is a wood to your right beyond which the path crosses a couple of pastures with the high park wall constantly to the left.

Oxwold House appears half-right but the path hugs the wall uphill, then around the poplars on the left and a small ash copse, emerging over a gate on to a narrow metalled road. Turn left and walk a mile into Barnsley. The park wall is still a constant companion and there are several gates through it to the left, all surmounted by the Baron's coronet, for Barnsley is the seat of the 3rd Lord Faringdon, Charles Henderson. There are also a number of different sized animal escape holes at intervals through the base of the wall so that the occasional fox or badger can pass into open countryside. At the final lodge take the centre of three narrow roads into the village, turn left along part of the Welsh Way then left at the B4425, returning to the Village Pub.

23 Mickleton
The King's Arms

Mickleton lies just below the Cotswolds in the northern extremity of Gloucestershire on the edge of Shakespeare's country and 3 miles north of Chipping Campden. The King's Arms is a prominent building in the centre of the village and is as imposing inside as it is outside. There are two beamed bars with open fires and walls in the local honey-coloured stone: there is a separate adjacent dining-room.

This is a Whitbread house which serves draught Flowers Best Bitter and Flowers Original, Marston's Pedigree and Boddingtons Bitter. There is Murphy's Irish Stout, Heineken and Stella Artois along with wine on draught, low-alcohol Clausterhaler and Kaliber. In the public bar you may play cards, dominoes and darts.

Food consists of daily specials, such as pork casserole, vegetarian dishes, salads, sandwiches and rolls, ploughman's lunches and a whole variety of attractive dishes from the blackboard. There is a separate menu for sweets. The pub offers omelettes with four fillings, six fillings for sandwiches and rolls and a couple of open sandwiches. The vegetarian dishes comprise vegetable crumble, crispy fried vegetables and Quorn and broccoli bake, all served with salad and potatoes. The main blackboard includes soup, mushroom pâté, gammon, venison,

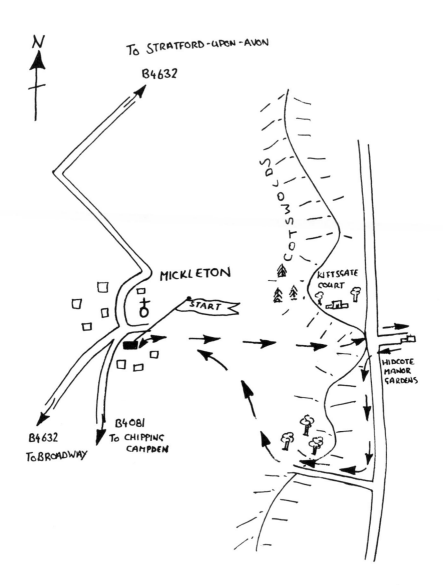

chicken and ham pie, Murphy's casserole, rump steak, and salmon steak. Puddings seem delectable: mixed Belgian chocolate ice-cream, King's treacle tart and home-made bread and butter pudding among them. The pub serves coffee, pots of tea and decaffeinated coffee. The inn has a simple, homely charm.

Telephone: Mickleton (0386) 438257.

How to get there: Mickleton is on the B4632 (formerly A46), 6 miles north-east of Broadway and 7 miles south of Stratford-upon-Avon. The King's Arms is in the centre of the village on the main road.

Parking: There is a large car park at the side of the pub next to the summer beer garden. It is also possible to park in the village nearby.

Length of the walk: 3 miles; it is possible to extend the walk to Hidcote Manor Gardens making the walk 4 miles. Map: OS Landranger series 151 Stratford-upon-Avon (GR 161435).

There is a great deal of variety in this walk, located in an area well known for its scenic beauty where the valley of the river Avon comes close to the Cotswold escarpment. In wet weather the footpaths near Mickleton can be muddy while part of the path up to the top of the limestone escarpment is very steep walking: come suitably prepared for both eventualities. At the midway point of the walk is Hidcote Manor Gardens, a National Trust property which is one of the most delightful gardens in England.

The Walk

From the pub turn right, passing the village shop and post office. In 200 yards, opposite Lloyds Bank, turn right along the lane beside the church. There is a waymarked bridlepath ahead across the pasture to a small metal kissing-gate and a footbridge over a stream. Walk over the field ahead, keeping the boundary some 20 yards to the right, to the point where there are four solitary oak trees. Take the stile and waymarked neat grass path ahead through the centre of a ploughed field, gently climbing up the foot of the slope. Cross the stile at the end of the grass track and aim for the conifers, keeping them on your left and walking over the brow of a steep spur. High above to the left is the house and park of Kiftsgate Court of which there are occasional glimpses.

The path now runs downhill to a gate and bridge with a stream tumbling down to the right. There is a waymark here and the path bends increasingly steeply up to the left in the foot of the valley. You aim for the lodge of Kiftsgate Court with its stone wall. Hidden from view there is a gate in the wall which lets out to the road. Walk ahead to visit Hidcote Manor Gardens, created this century by the great horticulturalist Major Lawrence Johnston. There is a series of small gardens within the whole, separated by walls and hedges of different species. Hidcote is famous for rare shrubs, trees, herbaceous borders and old roses. The gardens are open April to the end of October daily except Tuesday and Friday. It is ½ mile along the road to the entrance, but otherwise turn right at the lodge and take the road to the next junction where you turn right signposted to Mickleton. There is a wood and deep valley to the right and the road runs sharply downhill. Halfway down the slope go right on a footpath which is indicated as part of the Heart of England Way. In the right corner of the field ahead take the bridge over a stream and stile then turn sharply left through a gate 10 yards on. Walk ahead down the field, keeping the hedgerow to the left. Head for the gateway down the field, then aim for the prominent spire of Mickleton church. When you reach the road turn left past the church for the King's Arms car park.

Spare time to take a look at Mickleton village: the Tudor and Queen Anne houses are gems and the church is impressive. This was for generations the home village of the Graves family and they are commemorated in the north aisle of the church. The most famous was the 18th century writer and storyteller Richard Graves.

Northleach
The Sherborne Arms

The Sherborne Arms looks out on to Northleach Market Place. Parts of the inn date from the 17th century. There was originally an old forge in the dining area which was used by a local smith until 1970, when the blacksmith's shop and forge were incorported into the inn, consequently the building consists of parts at different levels running down the side of the Market Place.

Inside this homely and welcoming inn there is one bar, a separate dining area but also tables and chairs in the bar itself, which has a roaring open fire at cold times of the year. Examples of agricultural memorabilia and old prints line the walls. As well as a visitors' inn it is clearly a locals' pub, and both groups are made equally welcome.

The bar serves draught Flowers BB, Boddingtons Bitter, Bass, Hook Norton Bitter, Murphy's Irish Stout, Guinness, Heineken, Stella Artois, Gold Label and Strongbow cider, and low-alcohol drinks.

Food on offer is in a printed menu but the range of sandwiches and the daily specials will be found on a blackboard. There are four fillings for the ploughman's lunches along with a range of sandwiches and soup. You can have Sherborne giant Yorkshire puddings with Cotswold pork, hot and spicy chilli, mushrooms in white sauce and

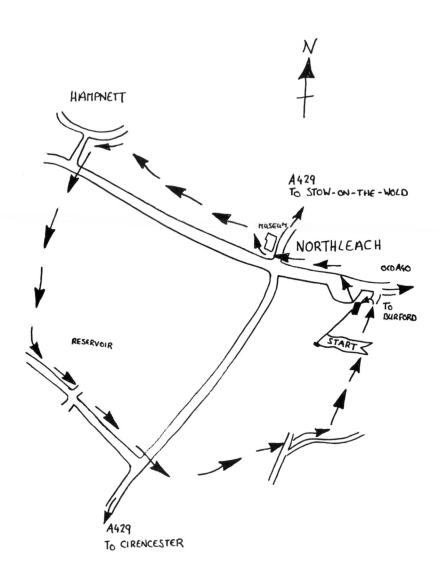

chunks of steak in Murphy's ale. Home-baked specials include lasagne, vegetable lasagne and steak and ale pie. Deep fried dishes comprise scampi, plaice, chicken Kiev and lemon sole. Among the grills will be found gammon, egg and pineapple, rump steak and pork chops with a range of desserts and tea or coffee to follow.

Telephone: Cotswold (0451) 60241.

How to get there: From Burford or Cheltenham use the A40 and turn off the Northleach bypass as indicated. From Stow-on-the-Wold or Cirencester use the A429.

Parking: There is ample parking in Northleach Market Place and High Street, also in the surrounding streets.

Length of the walk: 4½ miles. Map: OS Landranger series 163 Cheltenham and Cirencester (GR 113146).

This walk passes through the old market and coaching town of Northleach, and over the hills to the west and north of the settlement. Although there are some areas with relatively steep gradients, the large part of the walk is over the flat limestone atop the Cotswolds. This small country town grew up on the woollen industry. It has a splendid wool church with fine brasses and improvements made by wool merchants of the town and neighbourhood. In the 18th century Northleach was important in the coaching industry, being on the Cheltenham to London series of turnpike roads.

The Walk

From the Sherborne Arms walk across the Market Place into High Street and west along the former A40, called West End. You will pass Cotswold Hall of 1894 on the left then the modern fire station a little further along. Walk along the pavement on the right-hand side of the road to the edge of the town at the crossroads and traffic lights with the A429. Opposite is the Museum of Rural Life and its Cotswold Countryside Collection. Cross the A429 and just opposite the Little Chef café is a waymark and stile which leads round the side of the field and the boundary of the former prison. The building itself was erected by a local prison reformer, Sir George Onesiphorus Paul. It was designed so that the keeper could see all that was happening in the exercise yards without having to leave his quarters, and Pentonville Prison in London was a later copy of this design. It now houses the Lloyd-Baker collection of agricultural history, an excellent record of rural life. You follow the right-hand edge of the field and up the gentle valley with the stream on your right. Prison Copse is up the slope to the right.

In some 200 yards you cross over a bridge and follow the dry-stone wall and stream now on your left. Pass over a gate into a pasture, still keeping the stream to your left, then take a further gate and stile, clearly waymarked, which points the path over the centre of the next field and gently uphill towards the village of Hampnett which is visible on the skyline. Pass over a gate on to a concrete farm road and turn left down the road which goes downhill and curves round to the right.

At the foot of the slope, near to farm buildings, you cross a stream beside a sluice. Some 200 yards beyond the farmstead take the track to the left. Walk up the slope, through a gate and along a lane planted each side with young trees. The slope is still rising and as you come out of the copse, still with an uphill gradient, you will be joined by a dry-stone wall on the right. The slope levels out at the old A40, which you cross, taking the waymarked bridleway ahead which is level and straight to the underground reservoir ahead. There you will find a quiet country road along which you should turn to the left.

Walk ahead and at the crossing of minor roads continue ahead to the A429. Cross over very carefully and walk through the gate opposite on a waymarked footpath. Keep the boundary dry-stone wall to the left. You will be walking on a broad grass track which in due course curves to the left, passing Winterwell Barn on the left and farm cottages on the right. Northleach church tower is now visible half-left. Walk ahead down the farm road and exit over the minor road which you cross to take the waymarked public path opposite. This goes ahead but winds gradually to the left then the right. It is a broad track which could be an old enclosure road, possibly having also been used as a drove road.

Northleach church is now visible, an excellent landmark, directly to the left. At the point where the slope of the track begins a gentle decline, take the waymarked path to the left, keeping the field boundary and dry-stone wall to your left. Northleach is now spread out ahead over the convex slope and you take a stile ahead into a pasture and walk down the slope. The path's alignment is not entirely clear, but you should walk towards the hard tennis court to be seen in the valley bottom. Walk through a kissing-gate and turn left round a play area and beside the tennis court into a well defined lane. Walk along Meadows Lane and at the road turn left and return to the Sherborne Arms and Northleach Market Place.

Quenington
The Keepers Arms

The Keepers Arms is a splendid example of an unpretentious family-run freehouse. The welcome here is warm and genuine, both from the proprietors and from Fred, the friendly pub ghost. He has been known to do odd things in the pub, like altering the clocks or throwing the cushions around or even the saucepans in the kitchen. I was told that if Fred does not like you, then he will certainly appear. Needless to say I did not see him on my visit to the Keepers and the 300 year old inn remained undisturbed for another day.

This old-fashioned pub has two adjacent bars, the Keepers' bar and the Poachers' bar, and one room off for dining. No children under 14 are allowed in the bars, which are decorated under the low, beamed roof with brasses and country prints. There is a good display of clay pipes: these date from the time when a local would buy a pint, tobacco and matches and have free use of a pipe, which would then be collected and cleaned for use the next day. The pub also has an extensive show of mugs, jugs and decorative glasses. You can play darts here and use the electronically calculating scoreboards.

Draught beer served includes Flowers IPA, Boddingtons Bitter (the cream of Manchester), Whitbread BB and Whitbread Best Mild. There is also Murphy's Irish Stout, Heineken, Weston's Old Rosie Scrumpy and Strongbow. There is also low-alcohol Ame, White Label, Clausterhaler and Strongbow.

The Keepers has a lunch, evening and snack menu (no food is served on Sunday evenings). The wide-ranging choice includes jacket potatoes with a combination of seven fillings, seven varieties of sandwiches and six kinds of toasted sandwich. The lunch menu also has home-cooked egg, ham and chips, chicken curry and rice, grilled trout, fillet of plaice, scampi, six varieties of omelette, mixed grill, grilled gammon, and rump steak. In the evening there is a set menu with a wide choice within it including such dishes as salmon hollandaise, lamb cutlets, chicken cacciatore, prime gammon and peaches, trout fillets and rump steak with a variety of sweets and coffee. In summer you can take your meal outside the inn at the front where there are tables and chairs.

The inn has accommodation on a bed and breakfast basis, extending to three double rooms.

Telephone: Cirencester (0285) 750349.

How to get there: Quenington lies 2 miles north of Fairford and is best approached from the A417 at Milton's End, just west of the town. The inn is on the eastern side of the village green.

Parking: The Keepers Arms has a small car park at the rear but there is ample parking nearby beside the wide road which runs past the inn.

Length of the walk: 6½ miles. Map: OS Landranger series 163 Cheltenham and Cirencester (GR 145043).

For those who appreciate the unique beauty of riverine countryside, this walk is essential. It runs from Quenington alongside the mature river Coln into the picturesque delight of Bibury, surely one of the most beautiful villages in England. The walk leaves Bibury over the hill above Arlington Row and follows the outward route from Quenington in reverse. This is not just going back to Quenington the opposite way, for walking downstream opens up a whole new series of vistas.

The Walk
From the pub turn right along Church Street to the village green which you cross on the right-hand side. At the top of the green turn right along the road and go ahead over the crossroads towards Coln St Aldwyns. When you come to the river Coln bridge turn left before you cross it along an indicated bridleway which passes through a gate by the lodge. The public footpath is to the right along the riverside towards Bibury with Coln St Aldwyns on the opposite bank. Walk

104

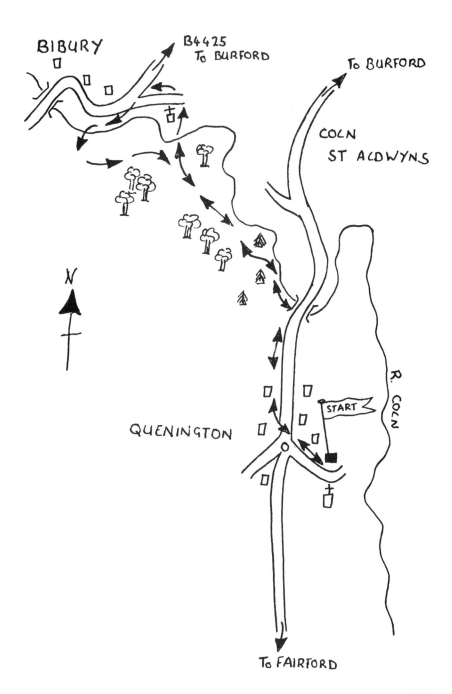

BIBURY

B4425
To BURFORD

To BURFORD

COLN
ST ALDWYNS

N

R. COLN

QUENINGTON

START

To FAIRFORD

through the gate ahead in a line of conifers which crosses the direction of the walk and you enter a wood of varying thickness and intensity to emerge in due course on a footpath with the woodland continuing on the left. At the end of the wood keep the field boundary on the left and the river bank on the right. Pass through several gates with waymarks here and there.

You may see coots, moorhens, wild duck and kestrels hereabouts as you emerge from a further woodland and turn half-left across a pasture. Take the gate and stile over a stream into more woodland where the footpath climbs quite steeply uphill. Emerging through a gate, you have a wall to the right with animal creeps here and there built into the base. A gate some distance ahead leads on to a track in an area well above the river valley to the right. The track runs half-right between walls and runs steeply downhill into the river floodplain.

Hereabouts there are good views up and down the Coln valley and in the middle distance the stone-built house which will turn out to be Court Farm. The opposite river bank is backed by steeply wooded hills which are particularly spectacular in spring and autumn. Pass the lodge to Court Farm on the right: a waymark takes the route along a road round a mill, granary and dovecote below Court Farm then crosses the river Coln. Bibury Court Hotel is to the left. This Tudor mansion was built largely by Sir Thomas Sackville in 1633 and is now a country house hotel with panelled rooms and four-poster beds. Join the road which passes into Bibury but close to the entrance to the hotel and near the telephone box take the footpath on the left through the upper part of the village. The church is on the left and well worth visiting. The Norman north and south doorways look out to prominent tabletop monuments in the churchyard, attesting to the earlier prosperity of this area in the woollen trade.

This is a pre-Norman church site. The present nave and chancel building with both north and south aisles and a dominating tower date largely from the 12th and 13th centuries. Decorated tracery in the windows was improved with money from the wool trade. There are a large number of aumbries for the safe-keeping of church possessions, Saxon capitals on the chancel arch, 13th century glass in the rectangular chancel window near the altar, a 13th century font, and a superb set of Scandinavian circle and pellet ornaments carved on the outside north wall of the chancel. Other such carvings from Bibury were moved for exhibition in the British Museum, for here is the best example of such work in Britain.

From the church turn left along the road with the river on the left. Opposite is a coffee and tea house, the Jenny Wren. Cross the footbridge on the left and follow the path over National Trust land which forms the Rack Isle wildfowl reserve. Arlington Row is on the left. This late 14th century row of cottages was occupied by weavers in the 17th century at a time when Arlington Mill was a cloth mill. The mill is now a museum with reconstructed blacksmith's and wheelwright's shop, collections of farm implements and carts, as well as items from the Victorian period.

Take the footpath to the left immediately before Arlington Row, walking up the broad steps, then turn left through the woodland, still rising but now less steeply. At the end cross a stone stile ahead. Keep the wall and beech trees to the left – you are now high above Bibury with the cricket pitch and pavilion to the right. At the end of the field take the gate on to the bridletrack ahead which affords a good view down the valley of the Coln. At the junction of tracks turn right and retrace your steps to Quenington, keeping an eye open for herons in the river and several cricket bat willow plantations close to the water.

26 Lower Swell
The Golden Ball

Situated in the heart of this delightful village, the Golden Ball is a traditional, lively and quite unpretentious village inn. It seems to be to a large extent a locals' pub, especially in the evening, but is also popular with passing motorists and walkers during the day as it is situated in rolling countryside in a charming corner of the Cotswolds, barely a mile outside Stow-on-the-Wold. It has a real fire and traditional pub games.

Inside, the stone-built inn has one main bar and three areas for drink and food, one of which is non-smoking. The garden with tables and chairs lies beyond the car park at the rear. There is a children's play area.

As a Donnington Brewery pub it keeps Donnington BB and SBA together with Weston's Dry Scrumpy cider and Gaymers Olde English Cyder, also Lowenbrau strong lager and Carlsberg lager on draught. The pub also boasts a wide range of Weston's ciders from the flagon.

Food is served between 12 noon and 2 pm, and 7 pm and 9 pm. The lunchtime menu is extensive, attractive and varied. Final orders are required by 1.55 pm at lunchtime and 8.55 pm in the evening session. There is a good choice of sandwiches on offer, with Cheddar or Stilton cheese, tuna and mayonnaise or cold roast beef as fillings. The ploughman's platters have honey roast ham, Cheddar cheese, hot peppered mackerel or Stilton cheese all with ample salad. You may also order prawn pitta.

Hot meals include such home-made dishes as Cotswold cottage pie and cheesy leek and potato bake, with basket meals comprising breaded scampi and chips and Wychwood spicy sausages. In the evenings the menu is extended to include a range of steaks, trout and chicken Kiev. Mouth-watering sweets include hot chocolate fudge cake and traditional bread pudding both with either whipped cream or ice-cream, summer pudding, chocolate ice-cream bombe and strawberry ice-cream sundae. Cheese and biscuits and coffee are also on offer.

The pub does not admit pets and maintains a strict non-smoking rule upstairs where it has three double rooms to let on a bed and breakfast basis.

Telephone: Cotswold (0451) 30247.

How to get there: Lower Swell is about a mile to the west from Stow-on-the-Wold along the B4068.

Parking: There is a small car park behind the Golden Ball. Alternatively, there is a layby just outside the pub at the side of the B4068, where the walk begins.

Length of the walk: 2½ miles. Map: OS Landranger series 163 Cheltenham and Cirencester (GR 176256).

Lower Swell lies in a green hollow of the surrounding hills, well watered by the fast flowing river Dikler. The return leg of the walk from Upper Swell passes alongside the Dikler and through some impressive parkland. A short distance from the first leg of the walk are several long barrows in and around the woodland to the west at The Tump.

The Walk
Turn left from the Golden Ball along the B4068, which is the village street. In 100 yards at the pretty war memorial turn right towards Upper Swell and right again in 30 yards. You pass St Mary's church on the right. It is built on a site which has yielded considerable finds of Roman pottery, coins, jewels and burial remains. The church has fragments of Saxon and Norman work but the bell tower was built in 1902 in memory of the Revd. David Royce who was vicar at this idyllic spot for 52 years.

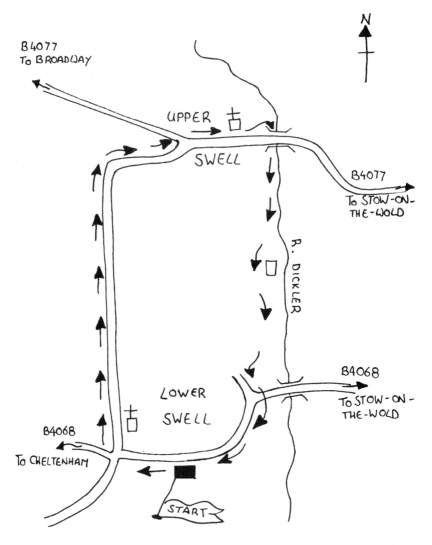

From the church the walk continues along the undulating lane, passing on the right obvious ancient ridge and furrow pastureland and extensive views towards Stow-on-the-Wold across the valley. Rolling farm and parkland contain excellent specimens of ash, walnut, beech and ornamental conifers, while to the left lie a series of long barrows near the woodland on the skyline.

When you reach the B4077 at Upper Swell turn right along the grass verge and walk through the village. Some care will be needed here and there as the road narrows and turns. St Mary's church is on the left. Just short of the bridge over the river Dikler take the footpath to the right waymarked as part of the Heart of England Way. You pass round the edge of horse paddocks with the tinkling river on your left. Coming to a bridge, weir and wood, turn right following the path through several kissing-gates. The footpath now broadens and soon enters parkland with a series of stately oak trees around you. The neatly maintained grounds of Abbotswood are to the left over the Dikler.

In due course the path descends gently to a further kissing-gate which gives out on to a well maintained drive from Abbotswood. Follow this drive through cottages, farm buildings and an old orchard and an ornamental dairy building of 1917, all part of the estate. To the left is a substantial lake on which you may see a flock of Canada geese. You exit from the driveway at the lodge and turn right along the B4068 through the northern portion of Lower Swell until you reach the Golden Ball.

Blockley
The Great Western Arms

27

The Great Western Arms lies towards the edge of this attractive and large village in the North Cotswolds, which is just to the south of the historic and pretty Northwick Park. The Oxford to Worcester railway line, built in 1853, is 2 miles north-east of the village and the pub takes its name from the railway company. In the mid-19th century there were some eight inns at Blockley, but none of them would admit the railway navvies so the Great Western Arms was built, then on the edge of the settlement, to accommodate and refresh the railway builders.

This is a Hook Norton Brewery inn and the pub has draught Old Hooky and Hook Norton Best Bitter; there is also Flowers BB and one guest beer a month together with Carlsberg lager and Carlsberg Export, also Murphy's Irish Stout. There is also low-alcohol White Label and Swan Light. Coffee is available at the bar. The pub has two bars and an adjacent dining-room. You can play darts and there is skittles at the top of the car park.

Food is served between noon and 2 pm, and 7 pm and 9.30 pm and there is a children's menu and a bar menu with sweets shown on a blackboard. The main fare runs from sausage, egg and chips through steak and kidney pie, lasagne, chicken curry, sweet and sour chicken and rice, cheesy cauliflower and potato bake, salmon and broccoli tagliatelle, rump steak, plaice and chips. There is also a variety of jacket potatoes, Cheddar or Stilton ploughman's lunches and seven types of sandwiches freshly made to order. The sweets are attractive for those who want to add the weight they lost on the walk. There is sticky toffee pudding, Black Forest gâteau, apple and sultana sponge and custard and apple pie; all delicious. You may eat in the bars, in summer in the garden or on the patio to the rear of the inn.

This pub has that indefinable Geordie warmth of welcome to it – especially so if you are a devotee of the round ball and a supporter of Newcastle United.

Telephone: Blockley (0386) 700362.

How to get there: Blockley is 3½ miles west of Moreton-in-Marsh. The B4479 runs through the village on which road the pub lies and it is easily accessible and well signposted from the A44 Moreton-in-Marsh to Evesham road.

Parking: There is an extensive car park at the rear of the inn where it is possible to park while walking. There is also parking in the village of Blockley.

Length of the walk: 3¾ miles. Map: OS Landranger series 151 Stratford-upon-Avon (GR 165350).

This is an undulating walk through extremely lovely countryside which affords panoramic views over Blockley and Northwick Park. Blockley has a history extending over a thousand years. It is picturesque, especially with the sun glowing on the honey-coloured stone from which so many of the houses and buildings are constructed, for the village is on a hill slope and particularly catches the morning sun. Take a look inside the church for it is a commentary on the centuries from Norman times.

The Walk

From the Great Western Arms turn left along Station Road and Lower Street, passing Lower Brook House bed and breakfast. Just over the brook walk up the indicated bridleway towards Pasture Farm. In due course the metalled road degenerates into a track running gently uphill over a cattle grid. At the barn take the waymarked footpath ahead along the field boundary which lies on your right, pass through a fieldgate ahead but cast a glance over your shoulder at the splendid view of Blockley on the opposite slope.

You will soon curve slightly to the left and come to the level on Blockley Downs with an extensive shelter belt of ash on the right.

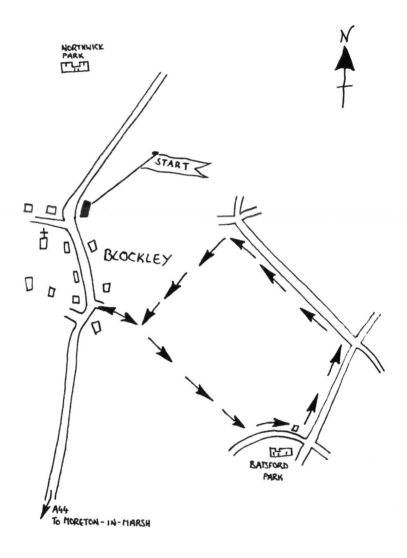

There is a gate ahead with the path waymarked. You now keep the field boundary to the left until you come to a further gate where there is no waymark: the path crosses the centre of the field, heading diagonally for the gate on the other side which exits to a road turning here at a right angle. Follow the road with Batsford Park to the right and descend Cadley Hill steeply through holly, ash and oaks to the estate yard on the right. At the crossroads turn left. Take a look to the right for a good view over to Moreton-in-Marsh in the distance.

At the next road junction turn left towards Draycott, undulating then plunging steeply down Dorn Hill. The beautiful pattern of Northwick Park unfolds ahead on the opposite slope. In those 300 acres Joseph Addison loved to walk and may have found inspiration for some of his essays. Northwick Park was the home of the Rushouts. Sir John Rushout was the most famous of them: Member of Parliament for 56 years, he was Father of the House when he retired in 1617. Also keep your eye open for kestrels hereabouts and note the splendid example of ridge and furrow in the old pasture to the right.

Just short of Draycott take the waymarked footpath on the left which goes up the farm drive and through the house garden on the left, passing immediately up the side of the house beside the stream. A gate and stile leads into a pasture with the path gently rising to the woodland on the right. There is a stile and gate over the brow of the slope. You head for the corner of the field ahead, keeping an old pond on the right. Go through a gate with the path waymarked ahead and in 500 yards to the left of a farmhouse, then in about 200 yards through a farmyard, over a cattle grid and on to a defined bridleway. Head for the barn ahead where you rejoin the path out of Blockley, bear right along it and retrace your route to the Great Western Arms.

It is worth visiting the church, extended in the 14th century, with a 15th century oak screen and chancel window, a 17th century clerestory, porch and pulpit, a chained Bible of 1617 and the Rushout Chapel of the 18th century with a splendid collection of family busts. In the churchyard is a curious memorial with a picture of a fish inscribed 'In memory of the old fish. Under the soil the old fish do lie. Twenty years he lived and then did he die. He was so tame you understand he would come and eat out of our hand. Died April 20th, 1855'.

Aldsworth
The Sherborne Arms

28

Situated away from the village of Aldsworth, the Sherborne Arms lies back from the main Burford to Cirencester road, in typically rolling Cotswold countryside, broken here and there by deep erosion through the limestone by one of the headwater streams flowing into the Leach and Thames. There are watercourses in the area but many of the valleys in and around Aldsworth are dry.

The Sherborne Arms is a family-run freehouse which is both friendly and welcoming. It is a cosy inn with one main bar and two substantial dining-rooms. Both darts and pool are available entertainment over and above the attraction of conversation. The bar has an open fire and exhibits rural artefacts round the walls, such as mole traps, sheep bells and horse harness. Indeed, it is appropriate that the horse is remembered in the pub for the old Bibury racecourse was nearby. On the wall of the dining-room are prints and mementoes of the course at Seven Downs, with a picture of the circular stand of 1800 for 'H.R.Highness, Prince of Wales, noblemen & of Bibury Club'.

Draught beer served includes Flowers BB and IPA, Whitbread BB, Castle Eden Bitter and Boddingtons Bitter. There is also available

Strongbow cider, Heineken, Guinness and Stella Artois. The pub also offers low-alcohol bottled lagers and coffee.

Food comprises bar meals, an evening menu, a special Sunday roast, and specials on the blackboard. The Sunday roast is lamb, beef and pork in rotation with vegetables and all the relevant trimmings, but from the other menus a whole variety of meals is on offer, from bowls of soup with bread to Persian lamb curry. Perhaps Bibury trout, grilled brill or fillet of plaice would appeal after a bracing walk, maybe home-made quiche, ham salad, home-made game pie, chicken and almond curry or a mushroom and hazelnut pâté. There is a front garden well back from the road where drink and food may be taken in summer months, having ample tables and chairs. Food is served between noon and 2 pm Monday to Saturday, but with a blackboard only on Sunday. Credit cards are not accepted.

Telephone: Windrush (0451) 844346.

How to get there: Aldsworth lies on the Oxfordshire/Gloucestershire border. From Burford follow the B4425 for 5 miles. The pub is on the right, lying back from the road just before the village. From Cirencester or Bibury also follow the B4425. The Sherborne Arms is 3½ miles beyond Bibury on the left, just after the turn-off to Aldsworth village.

Parking: There is a large car park in front of the inn. There is also parking space beside the road opposite the road junction into Aldsworth, very close to the start of the walk.

Length of the walk: 6 miles. Map: OS Landranger series 163 Cheltenham and Cirencester (GR 158099).

The walk offers the chance to explore some of the pretty countryside in this part of Gloucestershire. It is an easy 6 miles over gently undulating countryside, partly on quiet roads and partly on footpath and bridleway. On the whole the walk is through open countryside, but here and there hedges and woodland give shelter and variety and a greater chance to spot the wildlife.

The Walk

Turn right from the Sherborne Arms along the footpath which runs beside this relatively busy road. In 100 yards turn left along the lane signposted to Ladbarrow. The straight road goes right over the tops, gently undulating and with wide views and making easy walking. Lad Barrow is a round barrow off to the left some ¾ mile along the road and you might just see its site. You pass cottages on the right then pass under the pylons and wires of a high voltage power line. When I see

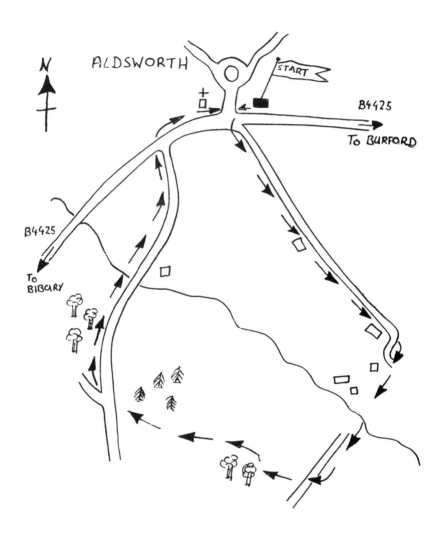

these lines straddling the countryside I think of them in John
Betjeman's terms as 'pendant bluebells', unsightly and inappropriate
though they may be.

Gentle undulations lead the road into a beech wood which has in
fact been imperceptibly rising all the way from Aldsworth. The
buildings and house of Ladbarrow Farm use the beech for shelter. At
the end of the road turn right, passing clever topiary on the left and
the east facing front of Ladbarrow Farm on the right. In some 100
yards turn right along a grass track through a gate with ash trees on

118

the right of the route. A series of gates takes the track downhill gently, then more steeply into Dean Bottom and Dean Farm. You cross the valley of the river Leach prior to Dean Farm and after passing through the farmyard emerge on to a hard road.

In some 400 yards a prominent stone-built house of Elizabethan vintage appears on the right, surrounded by yew hedges. Near the entrance to it take the track which runs half-right and walk ahead towards the beech wood on the horizon. At the wood follow the track round its north side then walk on a gently rising slope to the conifer plantation ahead along the clearly defined bridleway. Watch for the prints of deer: it is likely that they lie up during the day in the conifer plantation but you are only likely to see them near dawn or dusk. Some 400 yards beyond the end of the wood, having passed downhill into a dry valley which runs off to the right, take the gate ahead and turn right along the road in the lee of Bratch Copse. The signpost indicates that Aldsworth is 1½ miles away. Take this quiet road, passing asbestos and galvanized barns, then walk steeply down and up to cross the river Leach at Swyre Farm which is on the side of this sharply incised valley where the stream has eroded down through the limestone cap. Once more pass under the electricity wires to the B4425, turn right and walk carefully along it for ½ mile back to the Sherborne Arms.

29 Fairford
The Bull Hotel

The Bull Hotel is on the western side of Fairford Market Square. A substantial portion of the building dates from the 15th century when it was a monks' chanting house. The other part of the building is thought to have been a 16th century hall for a trade guild. The first record of the building being used as an inn dates from 1745, but by 1792, being situated on the Gloucester to London series of turnpike roads, the hotel was famous as a posting house, with stables for 30 horses, and the centre of a very thriving business.

Inside, the Bull has a traditional feel; the one large bar is warm, friendly and welcoming. It has low ceilings, open fires, an adjacent dining area for bar food and a separate dining-room for the full menu. There is also an adjoining residents' lounge which families with small children may be able to use for a drink and their food.

This is an Arkell's house, consequently Arkell's 3B and 2B are on tap together with Arkell's Kingsdown Ale and North Star Keg. There is also draught Guinness, Stella Artois, Carling and Strongbow cider along with excellent coffee. Before you decide what food to order, browse around the pictures, prints and old maps of Fairford which line the walls of this inn, then consult the extensive blackboards near the fireplace which feature starters, daily specials, light meals, specialities and sweets. You can have starters such as soup, garlic mushrooms and smoked peppered mackerel. Filled baked potatoes, salad, sandwiches or a ploughman's may form your light lunch.

From the Bull's specialities you can choose from sauté of chicken with Stilton, baked mussels or prawns, lasagne, bubble and squeak or home-made pie of the day. The fish menu includes the local speciality of Lechlade trout while the grills include gammon and steak. On Sundays there is a special roast meal on offer. Bar snacks are available from 12 noon to 2 pm and 6 pm to 9.15 pm but the bar is open throughout the day, except on Sunday when there is the usual break in the afternoon. Children are welcome and there is a non-smoking area.

Telephone: Cirencester (0285) 712535.

How to get there: Fairford is on the A417 Cirencester to Lechlade road and the inn is prominently situated in the Market Square.

Parking: There is ample parking space in the Market Square and surrounding streets.

Length of the walk: 4 miles. Map: OS Landranger series 163 Cheltenham and Cirencester (GR 153010).

Fairford grew up as a country market town with early-on a well established corn market and three annual fairs, but these came to an end in the 18th century. By the 15th century Fairford had become a centre for the wool trade. It was wealthy wool merchants who enlarged the church and installed the splendid stained glass windows. This is the only set of medieval glass which survives in its entirety: it illustrates the Bible stories vividly. This walk is along the banks of the river Coln and around the lakes formed by old gravel workings which border the Cotswold Water Park. It is a haven for wildlife and one would be ill-advised to attempt the walk without binoculars to hand.

The Walk

From the Bull turn right down the Market Square to the A417 which you cross, walking into Back Lane and Gas Lane. In some 30 yards turn right along River Walk, passing through a gate in about 100 yards along a well-made path beside the swiftly flowing, wide river Coln. At the footbridge continue walking ahead on the left bank of the river, passing through a stile and gate on to a broad riverside green walk. You cross a further stile, where the path can be muddy. In due course a kissing-gate takes the path into a pasture and follows the river bank with the village of Horcott spread out on the opposite bank. Further

121

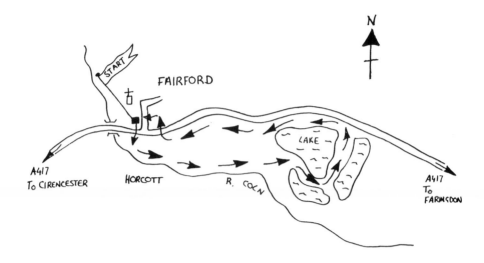

on you walk out of the field into a track beside the river with woods on the slopes of the opposite bank but with fields on the left bank. This is a good spot to view the ducks, moorhens or coots on the river and possibly see the vivid flash of a kingfisher moving up the stream.

At a junction of footpaths you continue ahead along the river, keeping the old gravel workings to the left. Soon a footbridge to the left takes the footpath to the lakeside along which you turn right. This is a broad embankment from which you can watch the swallows zip across the water of the lake. Soon there are old quarries to both left and right and the path uses a narrow isthmus between them.

The track now changes from grass to sand and gravel cover with a broad beach to the lake on the left. The path curves round the lake to the electricity wires with a waymark indicating the route along the direction of the overhead cables. This is an area of willow, ash and hawthorn with Fairford church way off over the lake to the left. At the end of the lake bear left round it, following the waymark. The A417 is on the right and the lake still on the left but the path is now a little distance from the water. Nevertheless you will still be able to view the water birds, swans and sometimes herons on or close to the water. RAF Fairford is just visible on the left over the rise beyond the lake.

You should now aim for the corner formed by a hedge as it abuts on to the field on the right. Walk keeping the hedge on the right, angling gently away from the lake into a hedge-embowered lane with trees here and there which overhang and shelter the pathway: this is an area of ash, elm, elder and hawthorn. On the right is an old railway embankment which formed part of the Oxford, Witney and Fairford

GWR line of 1873. At a junction of tracks turn right following the waymark, cross a gate and continue along a hardcore path into a long lane. At the point where a wall appears on the right take a left turn and at the edge of the settlement turn right, following the waymark into Beaumont Place.

You are now on the eastern edge of Fairford with the bowling green on the left and in due course a pretty row called Cable Cottages on the right, along with the Eight Bells Inn. Cross the A417 and walk into the lane opposite. At the next road turn left into The Croft, passing the small hospital on the left. Walk ahead into the cul-de-sac and a lane will return you to the Market Square with the church half-right and the Bull down to the left.

Great Rissington
The Lamb Inn

The village of Great Rissington lies on a slope between the village inn and the village church and manor house. It is a pretty stone-built Cotswold settlement with the ancient church and manor adjacent to one another at the foot of the slope. The privately-owned Lamb Inn at the northern end of the village overlooks the Windrush valley. The oldest part of this attractive building is some three centuries old and you will find a warm and hospitable welcome here. There is one large and one small bar. The larger room has ample space for meals to be taken, but there is also a separate dining-room.

Draught beers on offer include Hook Norton Best Bitter, John Smith's Bitter, Morland Old Speckled Hen, Beamish Irish Stout and Winter Warmer. Carling Black Label, Dry Blackthorn cider and Hacker-Pschorr premium Munich lager are also available. There are also low-alcohol drinks on offer together with specialist dessert wines, such as Elysium, a black Californian Muscat and Mimosa, a French Muscat.

Bar snacks are advertised on blackboards and include such fare as tuna and anchovy pâté, home-made soup, avocado and smoked bacon, shellfish pasta, home-made sausage and mash, and jacket

124

potatoes with five different fillings. There is also home-made lasagne, lamb curry and home-made steak pie. From the restaurant menu there is trout, roast duckling, roast guinea-fowl, turkey and Cotswold lamb, all freshly cooked to order. The Lamb has an extensive wine list and non-smoking tables in the dining-room: the discreetly quiet music is a welcome plus. There is a garden with tables and chairs for summer use; children are welcome in the small bar and while you are waiting for your meal to arrive you might like to examine the model gypsy caravan or the Great Western engine and coach which you will find in the bar. There is also a whole series of photographs of guide dogs, presented to the inn in recognition of their fund-raising for the Guide Dogs for the Blind Association. The Lamb has accommodation in 13 rooms ranging from those with four-poster beds, through king-sized beds down to single rooms.

Telephone: Cotswold (0451) 820388.

How to get there: Great Rissington lies within a triangle formed by Stow-on-the-Wold, Burford and Northleach and can be reached from the A429, A40 or A424, using minor roads.

Parking: There is a car park adjacent to the Lamb Inn but there is also suitable space in the side roads of Great Rissington.

Length of the walk: 4 miles. Map: OS Landranger series 163 Cheltenham and Cirencester (GR 200173).

The walk gently undulates down and back to the Windrush valley below the village. In wet weather the soil here can be muddy and clinging so that, as always, suitable footwear and clothing will be necessary. Great Rissington Manor opens its garden to the public, generally in late June and during the August bank holiday weekend. This is a four-acre garden with various trees and plants set around this substantial Elizabethan house.

The Walk
From the Lamb Inn turn right to the village green, walking to the right of it towards the church down the slope of the village street, passing on the way Clement's Farm and Charity Barn. At the church take the left turn, passing Woolpack Barn on the left. You will see a waymark leading up a lane to a gate and stile with a conifer plantation to the left and right. At the end of the plantation on the left bear left and follow the waymark which points diagonally over the field ahead. Go as far as a small triangular wood on the right. There is a waymark here which takes you on over the next field in broadly the same general direction. You should aim for the opposite field boundary some 250 yards from

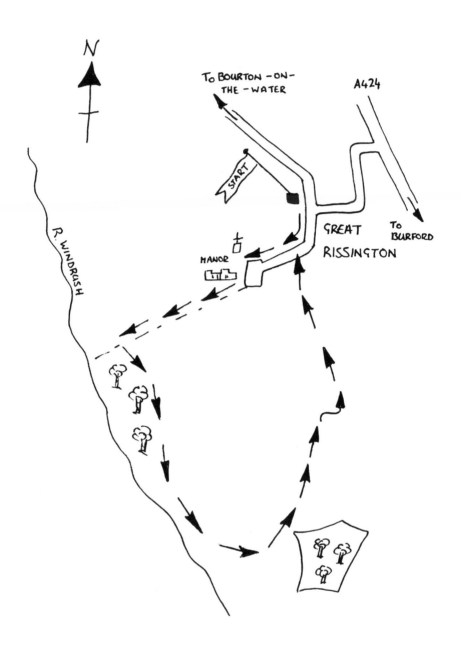

the right-hand corner of the field. Head for the prominent ash tree then bear right down the field boundary with the stream on your left. Pass by several oak trees on the left to the poplars ahead. Look carefully in this soft sandy soil for deer prints hereabouts. Walk into the poplars and turn left, following a waymark pointing along a grass track through the plantation.

The river Windrush is on your right and you might well disturb pheasant or wild duck as you progress beside the river and through the trees. You walk out of the poplars and over a stile and footbridge, taking the waymarked path ahead through an area of scattered hawthorns in grassland. At the end of the hawthorns bear left through a gap in the hedge, then turn right keeping the hedge on the right along a broad grass belt round the edge of the field. The Windrush is immediately to your right and you may see Canada geese in the fields beyond the opposite bank of the river. Scramble over a shallow ditch ahead. There are woods up the slope to your left and the river still on the right with a bridge crossing it. Near this point follow the field boundary left then right up the slope away from the river. There is a waymark on the left and in some 20 yards another waymark points you up the slope along a hard track with a wood of ash and conifer to the right. Go through the hedge at the top of the woodland. Turn left, following the waymark, initially on a track along the field boundary on the left, then in 100 yards turn right following the waymark over the field, the path rising gently into a clump of beech trees. There is a wood shelter belt to the left and the now well-defined track continues into the next field.

Near the top of the slope a waymark points left and you walk along the field edge with the boundary to the left. In due course a wood develops on the left. Pass through a gate and follow a waymark pointing ahead. The path now becomes a track, continues ahead and slopes downhill. There is undulating land over to the left leading down to the Windrush. You pass a wooden barn on the left and continue on the waymarked bridleway ahead which begins to rise gently with a woodland on the left. After further undulations, Great Rissington comes into view over the final rise. You follow the lane into the village. At its junction with the main street, turn right to return to the Lamb Inn.